"Exile-restoration is one of the central themes i
gives us a remarkably clear tour of the theme i
introduced to the theme of exile-restoration but will also be treated to an instructive survey of the storyline found in the Scriptures. Here is biblical theology at its best as a major theme is traced throughout the Bible, the intertextual relationship between the Old Testament and New Testament is illuminated, and the practical application of the theme is set forth."

Thomas R. Schreiner, James Buchanan Harrison Professor of New Testament Interpretation at Southern Baptist Theological Seminary, author of *Paul, Apostle of God's Glory in Christ*

"Matthew Harmon has produced a wonderful overview of a biblical theology of sin and restoration. This theological gem is full of insights that will be appreciated by a wide range of readers. Pastors, teachers, and students seeking to strengthen their grasp of biblical theology will be richly rewarded by their careful reading of this theologically astute and spiritually edifying exposition of these themes!"

Roy E. Ciampa, S. Louis and Ann W. Armstrong Chair of Religion, Samford University

"While distancing himself from N. T. Wright's view that 'exile' is *the* center of biblical theology, Matthew Harmon argues that sin-exile-restoration 'is a prominent motif in the biblical story line that plays an important role in structuring that story'. I wish this book had existed when I began serious Bible reading as a young adult! It skillfully, faithfully, and readably ties Scripture together from Genesis to Revelation and explains the heart of its message. It is exegetical, theological, and doxological in an effective balance. It dramatically depicts God's broad historic purposes since Eden and Abraham without 'obscuring the forgiveness of sins that the individual experiences through the work of Jesus,' an emphasis lacking in Wright, Harmon suggests. This is not the only book summarizing the New Testament's overarching message in concise terms, but it among the best. An added bonus is comments on application after every chapter and a masterful Recommendations for Further Reading that will benefit those eager for more."

Robert W. Yarbrough, professor of New Testament at Covenant Theological Seminary

"This is biblical theology at its best—what an outstanding contribution to the Essential Studies in Biblical Theology series! Matt Harmon combines well-crafted prose, careful exegesis, compelling whole-Bible synthesis, and timely applications for the church today. *Rebels and Exiles* not only informs readers about the crucial themes of sin and restoration but also stirs in us a longing for our true home."

Brian J. Tabb, academic dean and associate professor of biblical studies at Bethlehem College and Seminary

"A stimulating study of a central biblical theme. Matthew Harmon has his eyes on the biblical story line in which there is a pervasive sense of exile, but his eyes are also on the contemporary reader, who senses that something is missing. This book brims with exegetical insights and contemporary reflections, is well written and thoughtful, and is a profound reminder of the lengths to which God has gone to bring his lost sheep home. It is also a powerful reminder to the church that we are not home yet. I enthusiastically recommend it!"

Stephen G. Dempster, professor of religious studies at Crandall University, Moncton, Canada

REBELS AND EXILES
A Biblical Theology
of Sin and Restoration

MATTHEW S. HARMON

Academic
An imprint of InterVarsity Press
Downers Grove, Illinois

InterVarsity Press
P.O. Box 1400, Downers Grove, IL 60515-1426
ivpress.com
email@ivpress.com

*InterVarsity Press® is the book-publishing division of InterVarsity Christian Fellowship/USA®, a movement
of students and faculty active on campus at hundreds of universities, colleges, and schools of nursing
in the United States of America, and a member movement of the International Fellowship of Evangelical Students.
For information about local and regional activities, visit intervarsity.org.*

Cover design and image composite: Bradley Joiner
Interior design: Daniel van Loon
Images: geometric pattern: © kovalto1 / iStock / Getty Images Plus

ISBN 978-0-8308-5541-4 (print)
ISBN 978-0-8308-4382-4 (digital)

Printed in the United States of America ♾

Library of Congress Cataloging-in-Publication Data
A catalog record for this book is available from the Library of Congress.

P 25 24 23 22 21 20 19 18 17 16 15 14 13 12 11 10 9 8 7 6 5 4 3 2 1

Y 39 38 37 36 35 34 33 32 31 30 29 28 27 26 25 24 23 22 21 20

To Jesus, who bore my curse upon the tree.

CONTENTS

SERIES PREFACE

BENJAMIN L. GLADD

THE ESSENTIAL STUDIES IN BIBLICAL THEOLOGY is pat-
terned after the highly esteemed series New Studies in Biblical Theology,
edited by D. A. Carson. Like the NSBT, this series is devoted to unpacking
the various strands of biblical theology. The field of biblical theology has
grown exponentially in recent years, showing no sign of abating. At the heart
of biblical theology is the unfolding nature of God's plan of redemption as
set forth in the Bible.

With an influx of so many books on biblical theology, why generate yet
another series? A few reasons. The ESBT is dedicated to the fundamental or
"essential" broad themes of the grand story line of the Bible. Stated succinctly,
the goal of the ESBT series is to explore the *central* biblical-theological themes
of the Bible. Several existing series on biblical theology are generally open-
ended, whereas the ESBT will be limited to ten or so volumes. By restricting
the entire series, the scope of the project is established from the beginning. The
ESBT project functions as a whole in that each theme is intentional, and each
volume does not stand solely on its own merits. The individual volumes interlock
with one another and, taken together, form a complete and cohesive unit.

Another unique dimension of the series is a robust emphasis on biblical
theology, spanning the entire sweep of the history of redemption. Each volume

traces a particular theme throughout the Bible, from Genesis 1–3 to Revelation 21–22, and is organically connected to the person of Christ and the church in the New Testament. To avoid a "flat" biblical theology, these projects are mindful of how the New Testament develops their topic in fresh or unexpected ways. For example, the New Testament sheds new light on the nature of the "kingdom" and "messiah." Though these twin themes are rooted and explored in the Old Testament, both flow through the person of Christ in unique ways. Biblical theology should include how Old Testament themes are held in continuity and discontinuity with the New Testament.

The audience of the series includes beginning students of theology, church leaders, and laypeople. The ESBT is intended to be an accessible introduction to core biblical-theological themes of the Bible. This series is not designed to overturn every biblical-theological rock and investigate the finer details of biblical passages. Each volume is intentionally brief, serving as a primer of sorts that introduces the reader to a particular theme. These works also attempt to apply their respective biblical-theological themes to Christian living, ministry, and worldview. Good biblical theology warms the heart and motivates us to grow in our knowledge and adoration of the triune God.

AUTHOR'S PREFACE

AT FIRST GLANCE, writing a book on sin and exile may not sound like the most exciting topic one could explore. I will admit that when I began this project I shared a similar concern. But the more I explored how this theme is developed from Genesis to Revelation, the more I began to see the remarkable mercy and grace of God. I also began to see how Scripture speaks to the deep sense of longing I have for the new heavens and the new earth that consummates God's redemptive plan. And I was once again awestruck at the unity and diversity of Scripture as it tells the one true story of the world that makes ultimate sense of every other story.

There are a variety of approaches one could take in exploring the biblical-theological theme of sin and exile. My goal is to trace out this theme from Genesis to Revelation, paying attention to how the Bible itself presents and develops this theme. Thus, I have limited my engagement with what other scholars have written on the subject and have restricted what engagement there is to the footnotes. For those interested in pursuing this theme further, there is a brief list of suggested readings at the end of the book with a short description to help orient you.

Writing a book is a team effort, even when there is only one author. This book would not exist without the help of others, and it is my delight to highlight just a few of the people who have had a role in the process. My love for God's Word began shortly after my conversion at age thirteen, and it has been fueled by various pastors, teachers, and professors along the way. There are too many of them to mention by name, but I am especially grateful for the influence of Doug Moo and Greg Beale while I was a doctoral student at Wheaton College. Each in their own way has shaped my approach to the Bible, and those who are familiar with their works will likely find traces of their influence in these pages.

I wrote this book at the invitation of Ben Gladd, the editor of this series. We became good friends during my time as a doctoral student at Wheaton, and that friendship has continued to grow over the years despite the many miles that separate us. That friendship led us to coauthor *Making All Things New: Inaugurated Eschatology for the Life of the Church* (Baker, 2016), so I was thrilled when he asked me to contribute to this new series of biblical theology books. His friendship is an especially kind expression of God's grace in my life.

Books do not see the light of day without publishers and editors, so I am grateful for the many people at InterVarsity Press who have played their part in the process. Anna Gissing deserves special mention for her very helpful comments and suggestions in the editorial process. Her sharp eye and keen mind have made this a better book.

As a professor at Grace College and Theological Seminary, my interaction with students in and out of the classroom shapes what and how I write. I am grateful for the significant support I receive from the administrators, who annually grant me a reduced teaching load to facilitate my research and writing. Together we view this as a ministry to the broader body of Christ, and I am honored to partner with them in equipping people for faithful ministry in the local church, both here in the United States and ultimately around the world.

My family is a constant source of joy and encouragement, always asking me, "What are you working on?" as they see me sitting in my study surrounded by stacks of books and multiple computer monitors. Hanging out with my two sons, Jon and Jake, is always a nice way to recharge my batteries. Watching the two of them grow into young men is a delight to behold.

Words always fail me when it comes to expressing my joy and delight in my wife, Kate. She regularly makes sacrifices to enable me to have time to write even though she has her own full-time job teaching English. Even in the midst of the busyness of life, we remind each other that it is "us against the world." Truly your love is better than wine (Song of Solomon 4:10), and in the words of Mr. Darcy, you have bewitched me, body and soul.

Of course, without the staggering grace and mercy of our Lord Jesus Christ, none of these blessings would matter. Even though my sin had sent me into exile away from his presence, he restored me by bearing the curse that my sin deserved. "To the King of the ages, immortal, invisible, the only God, be honor and glory forever and ever. Amen" (1 Timothy 1:17).

As you read this book, this is what I am praying for you:

The Lord bless you and keep you;
   the Lord make his face to shine upon you and be gracious to you;
   the Lord lift up his countenance upon you and give you peace.
(Numbers 6:24-26)

ABBREVIATIONS

Bib	*Biblica*
BZNW	Beihefte zur Zeitschrift für die neutestmentliche Wissenschaft
CBQ	*Catholic Biblical Quarterly*
EvT	*Evangelische Theologie*
HeyJ	*Heythrop Journal*
ICC	International Critical Commentary
JBL	*Journal of Biblical Literature*
JSOT	*Journal for the Study of the Old Testament*
JSOTSup	Journal for the Study of the Old Testament Supplement Series
NAC	New American Commentary
NICNT	New International Commentary on the New Testament
NICOT	New International Commentary on the Old Testament
NIGTC	New International Greek Testament Commentary
NPNF	The Nicene and Post-Nicene Fathers
NSBT	New Studies in Biblical Theology
PNTC	Pelican New Testament Commentaries
PRSt	*Perspectives in Religious Studies*
SBL	Society of Biblical Literature
TynBul	*Tyndale Bulletin*
WBC	Word Biblical Commentary
WMANT	Wissenschaftliche Monographien zum Alten und Neuen Testament
WUNT	Wissenschaftliche Untersuchungen zum Neuen Testament

SIN AND EXILE IN CONTEMPORARY EXPERIENCE

HOME. JUST THE WORD ITSELF evokes a variety of emotions. In a basic sense, we use the word to refer to the place where we live. In other contexts, the word *home* refers to where we grew up or where our family still lives. But we can also use the term in another sense. Home is where a person feels a sense of belonging and identity. It is where we feel most comfortable and free to be ourselves. It's where we let our guard down and relax. It's where we usually feel the freedom to be who we truly think we are.

Yet there are people in this world that for various reasons are unable to live in the place they call home. For some that reason is voluntary. Many college students, for example, go to school far away from home. Some people travel far from home for work, spending days, weeks, or even months away in order to earn a living. For others, however, the reason is involuntary. Obvious examples are the criminal who is confined in prison or the daughter who is told by her parents she is no longer welcome in their home. Regardless of whether it is voluntary or involuntary, living in a place that is not our home is a disorienting experience.

There's a word for living in a place that is not our home—*exile*. Throughout human history, exile has been used as a form of punishment. The emperor Napoleon, for example, was sent into exile after a series of crushing military defeats. The apostle John was exiled on the island of Patmos by the Roman Empire because he refused to stop preaching the good news about Jesus Christ. Entire people groups have been sent off into exile by foreign powers conquering a land and scattering the native population into territories that are not their homelands.

But exile is not limited to those who are physically away from their home. Even people who are living in their homeland can feel a sense of exile when their beliefs conflict with that of the dominant culture.[1] From this perspective, exile "is the experience of knowing that one is an alien, and perhaps even in a hostile environment where the dominant values run counter to one's own."[2] In the broadest sense, exile *"designates every kind of estrangement or displacement, from the physical to the geographical to the spiritual."*[3] Defined this way, exile of some kind is a common experience.

Deep within the human psyche there seems to be an awareness that we as human beings were made for something more than we experience in our everyday lives. We go through our days with a sense that this current world cannot be what we were ultimately made for. There must be something that transcends even the best of what this world offers. We long for a place to truly belong, a place that is home in the fullest sense of that word.

This sense of living in a place that is not our home finds expression throughout literature and culture. A lighthearted example of this is the movie

---

[1]This concept is helpfully explored in Paul Tabori, *The Anatomy of Exile: A Semantic and Historical Study* (London: Harrap, 1972), 32.

[2]Lee Beach, *The Church in Exile: Living in Hope After Christendom* (Downers Grove, IL: InterVarsity Press, 2015), 21. For a survey of different studies on exile and its payoff for the academy and the church, see Pamela J. Scalise, "The End of the Old Testament: Reading Exile in the Hebrew Bible," *PRSt* 35 (2008): 163-78. See also Michael Frost, *Exiles: Living Missionally in a Post-Christian Culture* (Peabody, MA: Hendrickson, 2006).

[3]Susan Rubin Suleiman, introduction to *Exile and Creativity Signposts, Travelers, Outsiders, Backward Glances*, ed. Susan Rubin Suleiman (Durham, NC: Duke University Press, 1998), 2, italics original.

Terminal, starring Tom Hanks. Hanks plays Viktor Navorski, a man from the fictional Eastern European nation of Krakozhia. Upon arriving at JFK Airport in New York City, Navorski discovers that a coup has taken place in his homeland, and the United States refuses to recognize the new regime. As a result, Navorski is denied entry into America and is forced to remain in the international transit area. The rest of the movie recounts Navorski's adventures as a man without a country, living in no man's land as he awaits the resolution of the conflict in his homeland.

Although best known for *The Hobbit* and *The Lord of the Rings*, J. R. R. Tolkien made this keen observation about life in this world in a letter to a friend: "Certainly there was an Eden on this very unhappy earth. We all long for it, and we are constantly glimpsing it: our whole nature at its best and least corrupted, its gentlest and most humane, is still soaked with the sense of 'exile.'"[4]

This sense of living in this world with a longing for our true home is not limited to Christian authors. In two recent articles, Eric Grundhauser reflected on the following quote from Judith Thurman, a biographer and literary critic (who as far as I can tell makes no claim to be a Christian): "Every dreamer knows that it is entirely possible to be homesick for a place you've never been to, perhaps more homesick than for familiar ground."[5]

Based on this quote, Grundhauser asked readers to give examples of places they had never been, yet felt a sense of "homesickness" (or perhaps one could even call it "farsickness")—what the Germans refer to as *Fernweh*. The responses were fascinating as readers described their longings for places that were real and fictional. Several readers described longings for places where their ancestors originated but they themselves had never been able to visit for themselves.

Such longing for a place we think of as our true home is natural to our identity as human beings. Yet if we are honest with ourselves, we are not

---

[4]J. R. R. Tolkien, *The Letters of J. R. R. Tolkien: A Selection*, ed. Humphrey Carpenter and Christopher Tolkien (Boston: Houghton Mifflin, 2000), 110.

[5]Cited in Eric Grundhauser, "Have You Ever Felt Homesick for a Place You've Never Been?," Atlas Obscura, February 27, 2018, www.atlasobscura.com/articles/homesick-for-place-you-have -never-been.

immune to disappointment, frustration, and pain, even when we are in the place we call home. Even at their best, the places we call home in this life are never completely immune from the brokenness, pain, and evil that permeate this world. It is natural for us to long for a place where such realities are not present, where everything that is good about the place we call home in this world is elevated to an even greater degree of enjoyment and everything that diminishes our enjoyment of such a place is done away with once and for all. C. S. Lewis captures this desire well when he writes, "If I find in myself a desire which no experience in this world can satisfy, the most probable explanation is that I was made for another world."[6]

The idea of being "made for another world" might sound like the stuff of fairy tales, but what if Lewis is right? What if the reason we pine for a place we can truly call home—a place that is even better than the best this world offers—is that we as human beings were, in fact, made for such a world? And what if such a world actually existed?

But now we are getting ahead of ourselves. Before we can answer the question of whether such a world exists, we need to answer another question: How did this present world get so messed up? It doesn't take keen powers of observation to see that this world is broken. We are daily confronted with the realities of living in a world where pain, suffering, sickness, and flat-out evil seem to be all around us: mass shootings, a devastating cancer diagnosis for a loved one, someone you trusted betrays you, a person you love breaks your heart.

How did we as human beings get into this predicament?

Where did this sense of exile come from?

What happened to cause this state of exile?

What is the solution to this fundamental problem of sin and the exile that results from it?

Will there ever come a time when we live in our true home?

That's what this book is about. And the place to start in our quest to answer these questions is the opening chapters of Genesis. But before you turn there, take a moment to pray. Ask God to open your eyes to see what he says in his

---

[6]C. S. Lewis, *Mere Christianity* (New York: HarperOne, 2001), 135.

Word. Ask him to show you who he is and what he has done in this world to make things right. Ask him to show you how to better love him with your whole heart, soul, mind, and strength. Ask him how to better love your neighbor as yourself. And when you pray this, pray it confidently, because these are the kinds of prayers God loves to answer.

Chapter One

HUMANITY'S ORIGINAL REBELLION AND EXILE

WHEN IT COMES TO A GOOD STORY, the opening line is often memorable and draws the reader in. Take, for example, Charles Dickens's classic *A Tale of Two Cities*:

> It was the best of times, it was the worst of times, it was the age of wisdom, it was the age of foolishness, it was the epoch of belief, it was the epoch of incredulity, it was the season of Light, it was the season of Darkness, it was the spring of hope, it was the winter of despair.[1]

Or this famous opening from *The Fellowship of the Ring* by J. R. R. Tolkien:

> When Mr. Bilbo Baggins of Bag End announced that he would shortly be celebrating his eleventyfirst birthday with a party of special magnificence, there was much talk and excitement in Hobbiton.[2]

What about this more recent example from *Harry Potter*?

---

[1]Charles Dickens, *A Tale of Two Cities* (Philadelphia: Courage Books, 1992), 11.
[2]J. R. R. Tolkien, *The Fellowship of the Ring: Being the First Part of the Lord of the Rings* (Boston: Houghton Mifflin Harcourt, 2012), 29.

Mr. and Mrs. Dursley, of number four, Privet Drive, were proud to say that they were perfectly normal, thank you very much.[3]

These opening lines help set the stage for the story that follows and pique the reader's interest.

The opening words of Genesis are some of the most famous in the world: "In the beginning, God created the heavens and the earth" (Genesis 1:1). This line introduces us to the main character—God—and jumpstarts the story. It also acts as a title for Genesis 1:1–2:3, which lays out the six days in which God created the universe and the seventh day on which he rested. On each of the first five days, God speaks various aspects of creation into existence. Each day builds on the previous, leading up to the climactic sixth day when God creates humanity, his crowning achievement (1:26-31). Let's take a closer look at this important passage.

CROWNED AND COMMISSIONED

In contrast to everything else made to this point, God announces, "Let us make man in our image, after our likeness" (Genesis 1:26).[4] The concept of being made in the image and likeness of God is so important that it is repeated two more times in 1:27. In the ancient Near East, victorious kings would set up an image of themselves in territories they had conquered as a reflection of their glory and a reminder of their presence. In a similar (albeit far greater) sense, that is what God has done with humanity. God made us to be mirrors to reflect his glorious beauty to all of creation.

But there is more to being made in God's image and likeness than simply reflecting his glorious beauty. Immediately after stating that humanity is made in God's image, God blesses them and gives them a commission: "Be fruitful and multiply and fill the earth and subdue it, and have dominion over the fish of the sea and over the birds of the heavens and over every living thing that moves on the earth" (Genesis 1:28).

---

[3]J. K. Rowling, *Harry Potter and the Sorcerer's Stone* (New York: Scholastic, 1998), 1.

[4]By referring to himself in the plural ("let *us* make man in *our* image, after *our* likeness"), there may be a subtle anticipation of the triune nature of God, which is progressively revealed as Scripture unfolds.

In rapid-fire fashion, God gives five interconnected commands that describe his commission to Adam and Eve. The first three focus on God's intention for humanity to become so numerous that they eventually fill the earth. God commissions his image bearers to reproduce fellow image bearers. The final two commands center on God's intention for humanity to rule over creation. God is the great king who rules over the universe, but he has created humanity to rule as vice regents, mini kings and queens who rule under his ultimate authority. God exercises his rule over creation through humanity as they exercise dominion over all God has made.

God's purpose for humanity is to reflect his glorious beauty by filling the earth and ruling over creation as his vice regents. With the pinnacle of his creation now in place, God declares everything "very good" (Genesis 1:31) and then rests on the seventh day as the sovereign king of the universe (2:1-3).

SET APART AND UNITED TOGETHER

Genesis 1:1–2:3 describes the creation of humanity with a particular emphasis on their role as vice regents. In Genesis 2:4-25 the creation of humanity is told again but from a different angle and with a different emphasis.[5] The place to start is in verses 7-9:

> Then the LORD God formed the man of dust from the ground and breathed into his nostrils the breath of life, and the man became a living creature. And the LORD God planted a garden in Eden, in the east, and there he put the man whom he had formed. And out of the ground the LORD God made to spring up every tree that is pleasant to the sight and good for food. The tree of life was in the midst of the garden, and the tree of the knowledge of good and evil.

Whereas Genesis 1:26-27 focused on God creating humanity by his Word, here God gets his hands dirty, so to speak. He forms the man Adam out of the dust of the ground and breathes into him to bring him to life.

---

[5]Another distinction between the creation account in Genesis 1:1–2:3 and the one in Genesis 2:4-25 is the use of different names for God. In Genesis 1:1–2:3, *Elohim* is used, whereas in 2:4-25 the name *Yahweh* takes center stage. The shift may reflect a movement from God as creator (*Elohim*) to God as the one who makes a covenant with Abraham and his seed; see Bruce K. Waltke and Cathi J. Fredricks, *Genesis: A Commentary* (Grand Rapids, MI: Zondervan, 2001), 84.

After creating Adam, God places him in the Garden of Eden. But this is no ordinary garden. Based on the remainder of Genesis 2–3 and later texts such as Ezekiel 40–48 and Revelation 21–22, the garden was created to be the Lord's temple sanctuary here on earth.[6] It was the place where God walked with Adam and Eve (Genesis 3:8). The presence of the cherubim as guardians of the garden once the sinful couple is exiled further suggests it is a temple sanctuary (3:24) since they are later present in both the tabernacle and the temple (Exodus 25:18; 1 Kings 6:23-35). The abundance of botanical and arboreal imagery that describes Solomon's temple suggests that it was patterned after Eden (1 Kings 6–7), and later passages that anticipate the eschatological temple describe it in Edenic terms (Isaiah 60:13, 21).

But not only is Eden portrayed as the earthly sanctuary of God; the task that God gives Adam when placing him in the garden is a priestly role. According to Genesis 2:15, God "put him in the garden of Eden to work it and keep it." This same combination of the verbs *work* (which could also be translated *serve*) and *keep* (or *guard*) are used elsewhere to describe the role of priests serving in the tabernacle and protecting its purity (Numbers 3:7-8; 8:25-26; 18:5-6; 1 Chronicles 23:32; Ezekiel 44:14). Immediately following this description of the priestly role, God gives his priest, Adam, a command for him to keep—not to eat from the Tree of the Knowledge of Good and Evil (Genesis 2:17). Like the later priests who were entrusted with God's law, Adam was expected to obey it and prevent anything unclean from entering God's sanctuary. This observation will become especially important when we look at Genesis 3.

As a priest, Adam was charged with mediating the divine presence to all of creation. Humanity would be the conduit through which God would make himself known. Through his faithful obedience, Adam and his offspring would expand the boundaries of God's garden sanctuary and preserve its purity by ejecting anything unclean that sought to enter.

God did not leave Adam alone to carry out his priestly role. He created "a helper fit for him" by making a woman who corresponded to him

---

[6]On this important theme, see especially G. K. Beale, *The Temple and the Church's Mission: A Biblical Theology of the Dwelling Place of God*, NSBT 17 (Downers Grove, IL: InterVarsity Press, 2004), 66-80. This section is indebted to his work.

(Genesis 2:18). Adam's response when God presents the woman to him is worth quoting in full: "This at last is bone of my bones and flesh of my flesh; she shall be called Woman, because she was taken out of Man" (2:23). His excitement is palpable. God has given him a partner to come alongside him and fulfill God's purpose for both of them.

Thus, in addition to the royal role that God gives humanity to rule over his creation, he also grants them a priestly role. As kings and priests, humans were to work together to accomplish God's purposes in this world so that his glory would be on full display through his obedient image bearers.

REBELLIOUS AND JUDGED

This idyllic picture did not last long. Genesis 3 opens with the ominous note that "the serpent was more crafty than any other beast of the field that the Lord God had made" (3:1). By questioning the goodness of God and the truthfulness of his word to the first couple, the serpent deceives the woman into eating from the Tree of the Knowledge of Good and Evil, and she in turn gives some to her husband (3:1-6). Within moments the consequences of their actions began to sink in: "Then the eyes of both were opened, and they knew that they were naked" (3:7). Although their nakedness was not a problem before they ate from the Tree of the Knowledge of Good and Evil (2:25), now it was a source of shame, something to be hidden. In their desperation "they sewed fig leaves together and made themselves loincloths" (3:7).

Instead of welcoming God later that day when it came time for him to walk in his garden sanctuary, Adam and his wife "hid themselves from the presence of the Lord God among the trees of the garden" (Genesis 3:8). When God confronted Adam about whether he had eaten the forbidden fruit, he shifted the blame to Eve (3:9-12). The woman made a similar move when questioned by God, blaming the serpent for deceiving her (3:13).

Before looking at God's pronouncement of judgment, it is worth pausing to reflect on what has happened. Adam was commissioned as king, charged with ruling over creation by filling it with image bearers. But instead of exercising dominion over the serpent, he allowed the serpent to exercise dominion over him by listening to and agreeing with the serpent's slanderous invitation to disobey Yahweh. Adam was also commissioned as a priest, charged with mediating God's presence in the world, keeping his law, and maintaining the purity and holiness of his garden sanctuary here on earth. But instead of ejecting the unholy serpent from the garden and remaining obedient to God's law, Adam not only permits the serpent to remain in God's sanctuary but joins with him in his uncleanness.[7]

Throughout the centuries there have been many attempts to describe the sin of Adam and his wife. One of the more prominent ways is to classify it as pride or selfishness. After stating that pride is the beginning of sin, Augustine contends that pride is "the craving for undue exaltation," which is "when the soul abandons Him to whom it ought to cleave as its end, and becomes a kind of end to itself. This happens when it becomes its own satisfaction."[8] Another prominent way of framing Adam's sin is to describe it in terms of breaking God's covenant. Understood this way, Adam failed to fulfill his responsibilities as God's servant when faced with his first probationary trial.[9] Along these lines Cornelius Plantinga defines sin as "the smearing of a relationship, the grieving of one's divine parent and benefactor, a betrayal of the partner to whom one is joined by a holy bond."[10] It is also possible to frame sin in terms of "faithlessness on humanity's part born of a lack of faith in God's character and God's Word."[11]

While each of these proposals has merit, two particular ways of describing Adam and Eve's sin are especially relevant for our purposes. The first is rebellion. God made Adam to be a king who ruled under his authority, reflecting the beauty of the Lord as he exercised dominion over God's creation. But instead of humbly submitting to Yahweh as his sovereign, Adam rejected his authority by determining good and evil for himself. Instead of living as a

---

[7]Meredith Kline makes the interesting argument that God placed the Tree of the Knowledge of Good and Evil in Eden to lure Satan into the garden for Adam to execute judgment on him; see Meredith G. Kline, *Kingdom Prologue: Genesis Foundations for a Covenantal Worldview* (Overland Park, KS: Two Age Press, 2000), 121.

[8]Augustine, *City of God*, 14.13 (NPNF 2:273).

[9]See, e.g., Michael S. Horton, *The Christian Faith: A Systematic Theology for Pilgrims on the Way* (Grand Rapids, MI: Zondervan, 2010), 408-14.

[10]Cornelius Plantinga, *Not the Way It's Supposed to Be: A Breviary of Sin* (Grand Rapids, MI: Eerdmans, 1995), 12.

[11]Paul R. House, "Sin in the Law," in *Fallen: A Theology of Sin*, ed. Christopher W. Morgan and Robert A. Peterson (Wheaton, IL: Crossway, 2013), 45.

mirror to reflect the beauty and glory of his Maker, Adam sought that glory for himself. Instead of stepping in to exercise authority over the serpent and protecting his wife from lies, Adam passively sat by as the serpent undermined both God's authority and his. Instead of fearing the Lord and thus growing in true wisdom, Adam pursued a shortcut that led to folly. Considered from multiple angles, Adam's sin was an act of treasonous rebellion.

A second way of describing Adam's sin is idolatry. In the most basic sense, idolatry is loving anything or anyone more than God. The Lord created Adam to be a priest who mediates God's presence, keeps his law, and preserves the purity of God's garden sanctuary. His first priority was supposed to be complete devotion to Yahweh. But instead of cherishing the presence of God above all others, Adam prioritized the presence and approval of the serpent. Instead of keeping the law of the Lord at any cost, Adam believed the lies of the serpent over the truth of God's word. Instead of guarding the purity of Yahweh's garden sanctuary, Adam entertained the impure serpent and eventually joined in his evil ways. Adam's sin was a brazen act of flagrant idolatry.

As a result of Adam and Eve's rebellion and idolatry, sin now affects every aspect of a person's existence.[12] Our minds, our hearts, our desires, our inclinations, our wills, our actions, and even our physical bodies are all stained by the effects of sin (Jeremiah 17:9; Romans 7:18; Ephesians 2:1-3; 4:17-19; Titus 1:15-16). While the image of God still remains in every individual human being (no matter how sinful he or she is), it is marred, obscured, and distorted by the effects of sin. Sin affects not only the individual but also humanity on a social and communal level, shaping and distorting its various systems, structures, and organizations.

In light of this rebellion and idolatry, God's judgment falls swiftly and terribly. First on God's docket is the serpent (Genesis 3:14-15). Just as he is more crafty than all the beasts that God had made (3:1), he is now cursed more than any of them (3:14). Slithering on his belly and eating dust will be his lot (3:14). Even more ominous is Yahweh's assertion of perpetual

---

[12]This, in essence, is what the expression *total depravity* means. It does not mean that human beings are as bad as they could be, but only that there is no aspect of our being that remains unaffected by sin. In light of the baggage attached to the phrase total depravity, Plantinga prefers the expression *pervasive depravity* to express this concept (*Not the Way It's Supposed to Be*, 150-52).

conflict between the offspring of the serpent and that of the woman, which will culminate in the woman's offspring dealing the serpent a mortal blow, yet not without suffering a serious wound of his own (3:15; more on this verse below). The seeming "victory" of the serpent in overthrowing and defiling Adam, God's divinely appointed priest-king, will eventually result in his own destruction.

Next, God moves on to the woman (Genesis 3:16). His words are concise but devastating. The pain of childbirth will be intensified. Rather than a disposition that submits to the leadership of her husband, she will be inclined to undermine and at times even reject it altogether. Rather than live under the wise, servant-hearted leadership of her husband, the woman will be subject to the husband's sinful desire to abuse his leadership role.[13]

Finally, God comes to the man (Genesis 3:17-19). For Adam's failure to obey the command not to eat from the Tree of the Knowledge of Good and Evil, God places the ground under a curse. Rather than submit to Adam's authority as God's vice regent, the ground will resist his efforts to cultivate it by producing thorns and thistles. Adam is condemned to an existence of arduous labor simply to produce food. He will spend his life this way until he dies, when he will return to the dust from which he was created.

As awful as these pronouncements of judgment are, there is one more to come. The culmination of God's judgment is exile from the garden (Genesis 3:22-24). God states his rationale for this drastic action: "Behold, the man has become like one of us in knowing good and evil. Now, lest he reach out his hand and take also of the tree of life and eat, and live forever" (3:22). Apparently, if Adam and his wife had eaten from this tree after their idolatrous rebellion, they would have been locked into their sinful state forever. So God sends them into exile, away from the garden sanctuary where his presence dwelt. As Kline notes, "Defiled and driven out, the former priests of Eden were now regarded as themselves potential intruders, against whom the sanctuary must be guarded."[14]

---

[13]While some conclude that the husband's leadership is a result of the fall, the larger context of Genesis 1–2 suggests that God intended the husband to lead his wife from the very beginning.
[14]Kline, *Kingdom Prologue*, 137.

But would they? Assumes you only need one bite to [...]

The message could not be clearer: *rebellion and idolatry result in exile— separation from the presence of God.* As pure holiness, God cannot allow sinful humanity access to his garden sanctuary, so he drives the couple out.[15] To ensure that they can never reenter the garden, God places cherubim at the entrance as angelic guardians in conjunction with a flaming sword that turned in every direction. God ensures that humanity can never again access the Tree of Life at the center of his garden sanctuary. Yes, they are still divine image bearers. But now they must live out this reality in exile, away from the presence of their Maker. Meredith Kline aptly summarizes Adam and Eve's situation at this point:

Eden - the place where God is— is over home

> Driven from his native homeland, the holy and blessed land, into a world profane and cursed, man is in exile on the face of the earth. His historical existence is a wandering east of Eden, a diaspora. Until the restoration of all things, the earth has taken on the character of a wilderness, lying outside the holy land of promise. It is a realm under the shadow of death.[16]

Thus, it is hard to overstate the importance of this sentence of exile for the larger biblical story line. God's people have been ejected from the place he gave them and are cut off from his presence.[17]

HOPE IN THE MIDST OF JUDGMENT

Despite the dark overtones of judgment that pervade Genesis 3, notes of hope are also prominent. Four in particular stand out.

The first is found in God's words of judgment on the serpent. Yahweh's announcement of perpetual hostility between the serpent and the woman and their respective offspring means that God will not decisively wipe out the human race. But there is more here than mere survival of humanity. The hostility between the seed of the serpent and of the woman will not end in

---

[15]In Hebrew, this is the same verb God uses to describe what he will do to the nations inhabiting the Promised Land to enable Israel to possess it (Exodus 34:11).

[16]Kline, *Kingdom Prologue*, 137.

[17]Citing evidence from rabbinic sources, Roy Ciampa argues that the Pentateuchal context should lead the reader to see the story of Adam's exile from the garden in light of the blessings and curses articulated for Israel in Deuteronomy; see Roy E. Ciampa, "The History of Redemption," in *Central Themes in Biblical Theology: Mapping Unity in Diversity*, ed. Scott J. Hafemann and Paul R. House (Grand Rapids, MI: Baker Books, 2007), 259-61.

a stalemate. By all appearances the serpent has won this initial battle. Yet a day is coming when the seed of the woman will "bruise" the serpent's head; he will decisively defeat the serpent. But this victory will come at a cost, because the serpent will "bruise" the heel of the woman's seed. In other words, the seed of the woman will one day do what Adam failed to do (defeating the serpent and obeying God the great King), but doing so will result in him suffering a grievous blow. Sometimes referred to as the *protoevangelium* ("first gospel"), this promise of a serpent-crusher from the line of the woman was the foundation of hope for the human race from this point forward.

Second, despite the warning that in the day they ate from the Tree of the Knowledge of Good and Evil they would certainly die (Genesis 2:16-17), Adam and Eve did not immediately experience physical death. Yes, they died spiritually, but God allowed them to remain physically alive so they could be redeemed. Indeed, they would survive to become the parents of the godly line through whom the serpent-crusher would eventually come (5:1-3).

The third note of hope is found in the name that Adam gives to his wife immediately after God's judgment has been announced. He calls her Eve, a name that in Hebrew means "life-giver." To make sure that we do not miss the significance of Eve's name, Genesis 3:20 explains that Adam gave her this name "because she was the mother of all living." The significance of this name goes beyond Eve's role as the one from whom all subsequent people would come. It is also an expression of faith in God's promise that through her the serpent-crusher would come to obey where they had failed.

A final note of hope is found in God's provision of clothing for the couple. Genesis 3:21 says that "the LORD God made for Adam and for his wife garments of skins and clothed them." On one level God is simply replacing the hastily made fig leaf coverings Adam and Eve had made in the aftermath of their sin (3:7) with the more substantive covering of animal skins. But there is likely a deeper significance to this act. For God to provide the animal skins, he had to kill those animals. Instead of Adam and Eve experiencing physical death, God provided the animals as a sacrifice in their place. By providing the sacrifice to cover the sins of Adam and Eve, God establishes a pattern that not only continues throughout the Bible but also anticipates the definitive sacrifice that God will provide—his Son, Jesus Christ.

Despite Adam and Eve's idolatrous rebellion leading to their exile from God's garden sanctuary, the final word does not belong to sin, death, or the serpent. Yes, God's judgment—culminating in exile—falls swiftly and severely. But it is not the final word. Through the dark clouds of judgment stream rays of hope that God's purposes for creation have not been thwarted. Nonetheless, a fundamental pattern emerges: sin leads to exile. As we will see, this sin-exile paradigm becomes foundational for understanding human existence and the biblical story line.

SIN AND EXILE IN GENESIS

The sin and resulting exile of Adam and Eve establishes a pattern that is re-peated at numerous points in Genesis, albeit often on a smaller scale.[18]

In the aftermath of their ejection from the garden, Adam and Eve produce two sons—Cain and Abel (Genesis 4:1-26). When God accepts Abel's offering but rejects Cain's, Cain is filled with rage. Despite the divine warning that sin was crouching at his door, Cain—like his parents before him—is overcome by sin and murders his brother. In a scene reminiscent of what happened to his parents after they sinned (3:9-13), God confronts Cain. Just as Adam's sin resulted in the ground being cursed, Cain is "cursed from the ground. . . . When you work the ground, it shall no longer yield to you its strength" (4:11-12). And, just like his parents before him, Cain is sent into exile for his sin: "You shall be a fugitive and a wanderer on the earth" (4:12). Yet just as God showed Adam and Eve mercy in the midst of judgment, so too he shows Cain compassion. When Cain laments his fate as "a fugitive and wanderer on the earth," God promises vengeance on any who would kill him and places a mark of protection on him. With God's provision in place, "Cain went away from the presence of the LORD and settled in the land of Nod, east of Eden"

---

[18]L. Michael Morales, *Who Shall Ascend the Mountain of the Lord? A Biblical Theology of the Book of Leviticus*, NSBT 37 (Downers Grove, IL: InterVarsity Press, 2015), 49-74 argues that both Genesis 2–11 ("the broad movement from Genesis 1 to 11, then, is a descent from the heights of the mountain of God down to the depths of exile, from Eden to Babylon" [61]) and Genesis 12–50 display a pattern of movement away from God's presence into exile.

(4:16). By settling in the land of Nod (which in Hebrew means "wandering"), Cain acknowledges his identity as an exile, far away from Eden where the presence of God dwells.

In the generations that follow, sin continues its relentless and devastating march through creation. Things become so bad that God is grieved and decides to bring judgment in the form of a flood (Genesis 6:1–9:29). Sin permeated every aspect of creation and humanity, such that "every intention of the thoughts of his heart was only evil continually" (6:5). Yet to preserve the line of promise for the serpent-crusher, God shows favor to Noah. Through the ark Noah builds, he and his family are kept safe through the floodwaters of judgment. God temporarily sends Noah and his family into exile from the land while he de-creates the world through the flood. Once the floodwaters subside, God restores Noah and his family to the land and a new beginning— one might even say a new creation. Despite God's act of salvation through judgment, he acknowledges that "the intention of man's heart is evil from his youth" (8:21).

Notwithstanding the ongoing presence of sin, God blesses Noah and issues a modified form of his commission to Adam, establishing a covenant with creation (Genesis 9:1-18). He commands Noah to be fruitful, to multiply, and to fill the earth; but instead of issuing a command to rule over and subdue the earth, God announces that all the beasts of the earth will fear him and his descendants. To reassure Noah and his family, God promises never again to destroy the earth with a flood. Noah was restored from his exile from the land and given a new beginning.

But this new beginning did not last very long. Shortly after he emerges from the ark, Noah becomes so drunk that he passes out naked in his tent. Just as Adam's rebellion in the garden led to a state of shameful nakedness, so now Noah's sin leads to a similar state.[19] Noah's descendants continue in both Noah and Adam's footsteps of failure, rebelling against God and his purposes. Despite the command to be fruitful, to multiply, and to fill the earth, they gather together to make a name for themselves by attempting to build a tower that reaches into heaven (Genesis 11:1-9). In response to this

---

[19]Kline, *Kingdom Prologue*, 264.

act of idolatrous rebellion, God confuses their language and scatters them across the face of the earth. Once again sin has led to exile, and the intensifying nature of sin has led to an intensified form of exile.[20]

The pattern of sin leading to exile is also played out on a smaller scale in the lives of individuals in Genesis. After using deceit to receive the blessing of the birthright from his father, Isaac (Genesis 27:1-40), Jacob is sent away from his family (27:41–28:5). Joseph is sold off into slavery by his jealous brothers, ending up far away from his family in Egypt (37:1–50:26). While it is true that it was not Joseph's own sin that led him into exile, nonetheless the sinful jealousy of his brothers resulted in Joseph's exile from his family and the land of promise. Both Jacob and Joseph experience on a personal level the larger human experience of sin leading to exile.

THE PROMISE TO ABRAHAM AS THE MEANS TO END HUMANITY'S EXILE

Yet within this narrative of sin leading to exile, there is also the hope of restoration. After Noah and his family were exiled from the land through the floodwaters of judgment, they were returned to a renewed creation (Genesis 6:1–9:17). But as we have already noted, it did not take long for sin to rear its ugly head (9:18–11:9). While the line of promise remained alive, it was unclear how God would bring about the promised serpent-crusher who would obey where Adam failed and restore God's people to a place where his presence dwelled.

All of that changes when God calls a man named Abram. God makes a staggering promise to Abram (later renamed Abraham in Genesis 17:5) that reveals the means by which he will accomplish his purposes in creation and restore humanity. The entire promise is worth quoting in full:

> Now the LORD said to Abram, "Go from your country and your kindred and your father's house to the land that I will show you. And I will make of you a great nation, and I will bless you and make your name great, so that you will be a blessing. I will bless those who bless you, and him who dishonors

---

[20]Helpfully noted by Gerhard von Rad, *Genesis: A Commentary*, rev. ed., The Old Testament Library (Philadelphia: Westminster Press, 1972), 152.

you I will curse, and in you all the families of the earth shall be blessed."
(Genesis 12:1-3)[21]

This promise can be divided into three basic though closely interrelated
categories: people, place, and presence.[22] Together these three categories
of people, place, and presence indicate in nascent form how God will
restore sinful humanity from the exile that their rebellious idolatry caused.
Morales notes that "Abram was called out of Ur of the Chaldeans *for the
sake of the nations* who had been scattered from the Presence of God. It
is the return from *this* exile, itself a reflex of humanity's expulsion from
Eden, for which God covenants with Abram."[23] Because of their importance,
we will look at how each of these three promises is developed in the remainder of the Pentateuch.[24]

People. The first promise made to Abram was that of offspring.[25] To understand this thread, we first need to look back at the opening chapters of Genesis
and then look forward to see how the promise of offspring is developed.

God had promised hostility between the offspring of the serpent and the
offspring of the woman (Genesis 3:15). The offspring of the woman will defeat
the serpent, though not without suffering a significant blow from the serpent.
This offspring will obey where Adam and Eve failed, while at the same time
suffering the penalty for their failure. From Genesis 3:15 forward, the story
line focuses on the line through which this serpent-crusher will come, fun-
neling down to Noah and then continuing on through his son Shem (which

---

[21]The five references to bless/blessing in this promise may directly correspond to the five references
to curse/cursing in Genesis 1-11; see William J. Dumbrell, *Covenant and Creation: An Old Testament Covenantal Theology*, rev. ed. (Exeter, Devon, UK: Paternoster, 2013), 71.

[22]These categories are borrowed and adapted from Stephen G. Dempster, *Dominion and Dynasty:
A Biblical Theology of the Hebrew Bible*, NSBT 15 (Downers Grove, IL: InterVarsity Press, 2003),
74-92. Dempster uses the pairs dominion and dynasty, land and line, and geography and genealogy interchangeably.

[23]Morales, *Who Shall Ascend*, 68, italics original.

[24]The chapters in Genesis that follow seem to follow this division of the promise into place and
people, with chapters 12-14 focusing on the land and chapters 15-22 focusing on Abram's line;
see Dempster, *Dominion and Dynasty*, 77-85. The theme of God's presence is a constant motif
that informs both people and place.

[25]In Hebrew the term for offspring/seed (*zera'*) is a collective singular, meaning that it can refer
to either an individual seed/offspring or a group of them. Only the context can distinguish which
is in view, and there are places where both may be intended (e.g., Genesis 3:15).

means "Name"). His lengthy genealogy (Genesis 11:10-26) culminates in the birth of Terah, whose own genealogy immediately follows (Genesis 11:27-30). This brief genealogy introduces us to Abram, to whom God makes his staggering promise (Genesis 12:1-3).Thus, through the promise to Abram, God will bring the promised serpent-crusher who will restore humanity from its exile.

In the chapters that follow, the promise of offspring has both a singular and plural referent. While the plural sense of offspring dominates, at least two passages emphasize that the promise will come through a singular, individual seed. The first is Genesis 17, where God reaffirms his promise to multiply Abram's offspring and thus make him the father of many nations (Genesis 17:1-8). Here, then, the offspring in view are clearly plural. But after giving circumcision as a sign of this covenant (Genesis 17:9-14), God promises to give Abraham a son by his barren wife, Sarah (Genesis 17:15-21). God will fulfill his promise through the birth of this individual offspring, whom he is to name Isaac. The promise of many offspring hinges on a singular offspring through whom the blessings are passed on.[26]

Genesis 22 is the second passage that highlights a singular offspring. God tests Abraham by commanding him to sacrifice Isaac (Genesis 22:1-8). Just as Abraham is about to plunge the knife into his son, the angel of the Lord stays his hand (Genesis 22:9-14). After reaffirming his promise of numerous offspring (Genesis 22:15-17), Yahweh says, "Your offspring shall possess the gate of his enemies" (Genesis 22:17).[27] The promise of countless offspring hinges on a singular offspring who will defeat the enemies of God's people. Through Isaac, Abraham's only son, the promises find their fulfillment and result in blessing to the nations.

Thus, God's promise to Abraham is the means by which he will multiply his people throughout the earth. But the fulfillment hinges on the arrival of

---

[26]As we will see later, Paul picks up on this relationship between the singular and plural offspring in Galatians 3:15-29.

[27]Although most English versions have "their enemies," the Hebrew reads "his enemies" ('ōyəbāyw). For a convincing defense of reading this text as referring to a singular seed, see T. Desmond Alexander, "Further Observations on the Term 'Seed' in Genesis," *TynBul* 48 (1997): 363-67; and Paul R. Williamson, *Abraham, Israel, and the Nations: The Patriarchal Promise and Its Covenantal Development in Genesis*, JSOTSup 315 (Sheffield, UK: Sheffield Academic Press, 2000), 248-50.

who will one day obey where Adam failed, suffer for the sins
and crush the serpent.

Place. When God commands Abram to leave his family for a land that he
will show him, he is promising a place where he will dwell with his people.
For the first time since God exiled Adam and Eve from Eden, he will provide
a home for his people. Despite living in the land, God tells Abram that his
descendants will be sojourners and servants in another land for four hundred
years, until the sin of the current occupants is complete and God brings
judgment on them (15:13-16). The Canaanites' sin will result in their exile
from the land to make room for Abraham's descendants.

As the years pass, God expands the land promise to extend beyond Canaan
to eventually encompass the entire world.[28] The first hint is the varying descriptions of the geographic boundaries of the Promised Land throughout
the Pentateuch (cf., e.g., Genesis 15:18-21; Exodus 23:31-33; Numbers 34:1-12;
Deuteronomy 1:7; 11:24; 34:1-4; Joshua 1:2-4). Such variety suggests the borders
of the land are intended to expand as Israel dwells there and exercises dominion over it and the surrounding nations. A second indication is that God
promised Abram descendants more numerous than the stars in the sky or
the dust of the earth (Genesis 13:16; 15:5). Even allowing for the possibility
of hyperbole, the sheer number of descendants envisioned seems to demand
a larger territory than the land of Canaan. A third indication comes from
Romans 4:13, where Paul asserts that God promised Abraham and his offspring that he "would be heir of the world." The apostle, following the lead
of the prophets, sees in nascent form a promise that encompassed all of
creation.[29] The frequent descriptions of the fertility and fecundity of the land
portray it as a new Edenic Paradise where God's original purposes for creation
will be realized.[30] Lastly, the rest that God promises Abraham's offspring will

---

[28]Here I am largely following Oren R. Martin, *Bound for the Promised Land: The Land Promise in
God's Redemptive Plan*, NSBT 34 (Downers Grove, IL: InterVarsity Press, 2015), 71-74. See also
T. Desmond Alexander, *From Paradise to the Promised Land: An Introduction to the Pentateuch*,
2nd ed. (Grand Rapids, MI: Baker Books, 2002), 129-42.

[29]Martin notes, "Of particular importance is Genesis 26:3-4, where the plural 'lands,' when
juxtaposed with Genesis 22:17-28, reveals that Abraham's seed will possess or inherit the gate of
his enemies," *Bound for the Promised Land*, 73.

[30]See further Martin, *Bound for the Promised Land*, 83-84. Martin notes the following texts where
this imagery is drawn from: (1) the goodness of the land (Deuteronomy 1:25, 35; 3:25; 4:21-22;

experience in the land recalls what God intended humanity to experience as they dwelled with him in Eden (Exodus 33:14; Deuteronomy 3:20; 12:9-10; 25:19). Even while they were living in Canaan, Abraham and his offspring viewed themselves as strangers and exiles anticipating a heavenly city and country that God had prepared for them (Hebrews 11:8-16).

God's promise of a place to Abraham and his offspring is a promise to give humanity a new Edenic home where he will dwell with them. Sin does lead to exile, but exile is not the final word for God's covenant people.

Presence. Although not explicit in Genesis 12:1-3, the rest of Genesis reveals this element of the promise.[31] The first hint comes in Genesis 15, where Yahweh reassures Abram, "Fear not, Abram, I am your shield; your reward shall be very great" (Genesis 15:1). As Abram's shield, God is promising to protect him, which hints at his presence with Abram. In Genesis 17:1, God says to Abram, "I am God Almighty; walk before me, and be blameless." The expression "before me" could instead be rendered "in my presence"; Abram is commanded to live his life blamelessly in God's presence. God reinforces this promise when he says of Abraham's descendants, "I will be their God" (Genesis 17:8). The remainder of Abraham's life repeatedly demonstrates that God was with him.

The promise of God's presence becomes more explicit in the lives of Isaac, Jacob, and Joseph. When famine strikes the land, God warns Isaac not to go down to Egypt. Instead, Isaac should remain in the land because God has promised to be with him, a promise that is connected to the promises of place and people (Genesis 26:3-4). God then reassures Isaac in Beersheba by reiterating his presence with him, giving him confidence that he can remain in the land despite being surrounded by enemies (Genesis 26:17-25). As Jacob travels to see his uncle Laban, Yahweh reassures him that his presence will be with him wherever he goes to protect and provide for him (Genesis 28:13-16; cf. 31:1; 32:22-32; 46:4). The defining mark of Joseph and the reason for his

---

6:18; 8:7, 10; 9:6; 11:17); (2) abundant fruitfulness (Deuteronomy 7:13; 28:4); (3) fruit of the womb being blessed (Deuteronomy 7:13; 28:3-5, 11); (4) no barrenness (Exodus 23:26; Leviticus 26:9; Deuteronomy 7:14; 28:4, 11). Note also the frequent description of the land as flowing with milk and honey (e.g. Exodus 3:8, 17; 13:5; Numbers 13:27; Deuteronomy 6:3; Joshua 5:6) portrays it as lush and fecund, like the garden before it.

[31]As Ciampa notes, "Much of the theology of the Pentateuch has to do with the issue of the presence of God," "History of Redemption," 267-68.

success is that God is with him (Genesis 39:2-3; 48:21); indeed it is so apparent that even the pagans around him notice it (Genesis 41:38). Genesis even closes with Joseph promising from his deathbed that God will visit his people and return them to the Promised Land (Genesis 50:22-26).

People, place, and presence. What humanity lost through Adam and Eve's rebellion in the garden will be regained through the promise made to Abraham and his descendants.

CONCLUSION AND APPLICATION

As Genesis draws to a close, Abraham's descendants through the line of promise, extending through Isaac, then Jacob and his twelve sons, number seventy people. They dwell outside of the Promised Land in Egypt, in exile, as it were. But now the stage is set for God to accelerate the fulfillment of the Abrahamic promise of people, place, and presence, and in doing so to bring humanity one step closer to redemption, out of its exile away from the presence of God.

Even though we are a long way from the events described in Genesis, we experience their effects to this day. We sense that we are made for more than the everyday, often mundane existence that we experience. That's because we are! As divine image bearers, we are still capable of reflecting God's character by the way we relate to people around us. We can represent God's priorities and values in our everyday activities. We can rule over creation by bringing chaos into order. Every human being is made in God's image, regardless of gender, ethnicity, age, socioeconomic status, or any of the other ways that we make distinctions between people. This reality gives value and dignity to every person. It also gives meaning and purpose to our lives.

Yet we also experience the devastating effects of sin. We see it all around us. Seemingly on a daily basis we hear about terrorist attacks, political scandals, human trafficking, and countless other large-scale expressions of evil. Closer to home, we feel the effects of sin in broken relationships, economic hardship, sickness, and many other ways. More troubling is that we experience the effects of sin in our lives, infecting our thoughts, beliefs, attitudes, emotions, speech, and actions. Even our best efforts to do good in this world are often met with resistance, and our motives are never completely pure in any of our attempts.

The good news is that God has taken decisive action to bring restoration through his announcement of a serpent-crusher and the promise to Abraham. That is where our hope rests to this day.

Chapter Two

THE THREAT OF EXILE
IF/WHEN ISRAEL REBELS

AS ANY GOOD PARENT KNOWS, warnings and threats are sometimes a necessary and useful tool. Actions that seem insignificant to a small child may in fact be dangerous, such as running out into a busy street. The child may even "get away with" running into the street, unintentionally timing it when no cars are coming. But the wise parent understands that if a child regularly runs out into a busy street, it is only a matter of time before disaster strikes. Hence the repeated and sometimes stern warnings a parent gives to children not to run into the street.

In a similar fashion, as the ultimate Father, God repeatedly warns his people about the dangers of disobeying him. He makes it clear to them that if they rebel against him and pursue other gods, he will bring judgment on them. These warnings are so numerous throughout the Old Testament that we will devote this entire chapter to them, and in the next chapter we will look at the various descriptions of the exile itself. But to set the stage for God's repeated warnings, we first need to pick up where we left off in the story.

THE FAMILY THAT BECAME A NATION

Exodus 1:1-4 resumes where Genesis ended. Jacob, his twelve sons, and their families have migrated to Egypt: seventy people in total (Exodus 1:5). In the generations that followed, "the people of Israel were fruitful and increased greatly; they multiplied and grew exceedingly strong, so that the land was filled with them" (Exodus 1:7). God had promised to multiply Abraham's descendants into a great nation (Genesis 12:1-3), which in turn was God's way of fulfilling humanity's original commission as image bearers to fill the earth and rule over it under God's authority (1:26-28).[1] But instead of this fruitful multiplication taking place in the Promised Land—which itself was intended as a new Eden for God's people—it is taking place while Israel languishes in a foreign land under a foreign ruler: Egypt and its Pharaoh (Exodus 1:7-22).

As the years pass and the oppression worsens, God remembers his covenant with Abraham, Isaac, and Jacob (Exodus 2:24-25). He raises up Moses to deliver Israel from their bondage in Egypt (Exodus 3:1–4:31). God's plan is to bring them out of Egypt and lead them into "a good and broad land, a land flowing with milk and honey" (Exodus 3:8). The land God had promised to Abraham more than four hundred years previously (Genesis 15:18-21) would finally become the home of God's people.

But escaping their Egyptian bondage would not be easy. Humanly speaking, it was impossible. Pharaoh stubbornly refuses to let the people of Israel go and instead increases their workload (Exodus 5:1-22). God unleashes a series of plagues that simultaneously display his glory (9:16) and bring judgment on the false gods of the Egyptians (12:12). These plagues culminate in God killing the firstborn sons of the Egyptians while passing over the firstborn of the Israelites (11:1–12:29). Although Pharaoh initially sends the Israelites away (12:31-40), he soon changes his mind and sends his forces to pursue them to the edge of the Red Sea (14:1-20). Just when it seems the Egyptians have the Israelites cornered, God parts the Red Sea for Israel to cross (14:21-22). But when the Egyptians try to follow Israel across, God drowns them in the sea (14:23-31). In the song that celebrates this victory, it becomes clear that

---

[1] On these connections, see W. Ross Blackburn, *The God Who Makes Himself Known: The Missionary Heart of the Book of Exodus*, NSBT 28 (Downers Grove, IL: InterVarsity Press, 2012), 28-31.

a central goal of the exodus is "the building of the Edenic sanctuary so that the Lord can dwell with his people" (see 15:17).[2] Israel has finally escaped their Egyptian bondage, but their difficulties are far from over.

When Israel arrives at Mount Sinai three months later, God forms Abraham's family into a nation. After reminding them of what he has done for them, God speaks this promise to them:

> "Now therefore, if you will indeed obey my voice and keep my covenant, you shall be my treasured possession among all peoples, for all the earth is mine; and you shall be to me a kingdom of priests and a holy nation." These are the words that you shall speak to the people of Israel. (Exodus 19:5-6)

Despite being the Lord of all the nations, God sets the nation of Israel apart as his prized possession. By setting them apart as a kingdom of priests, God is commissioning them to live out a modified form of his commission to Adam to rule over creation and mediate his presence to the world (Genesis 1-2).[3] Israel's commission is also the development of God's promise to Abraham of people, place, and presence (12:1-3). God's plan to bring the serpent-crusher and fulfill his purposes for creation through a descendant of Eve (3:15) and the family of Abraham (12:1-3) has entered a new phase.[4]

In the chapters that follow, God lays out the various laws that will govern his covenant with Israel (Exodus 19-31). Although God gives the initial Ten Commandments to the entire nation, he calls Moses up on the mountain to give him the remaining stipulations. After Moses has been gone several weeks, the people become restless and make a disastrous choice (32:1-6). Like Adam and Eve before them, the Israelites rebel against God's authority over them. Instead of submitting to what God said was good and evil, the Israelites determine right and wrong for themselves. Rather than fearing Yahweh and submitting to his revealed wisdom, Israel walks the path of Adam's foolish rebellion.

---

[2] Stephen G. Dempster, *Dominion and Dynasty: A Biblical Theology of the Hebrew Bible*, NSBT 15 (Downers Grove, IL: InterVarsity Press, 2003), 100.

[3] Blackburn (*God Who Makes Himself Known*, 87) refers to Exodus 19:4-6 as Israel's mission statement.

[4] For a similar connection between this passage and Genesis 1-2 and Genesis 12, see William J. Dumbrell, *Covenant and Creation: An Old Testament Covenantal Theology*, rev. ed. (Exeter, Devon, UK: Paternoster, 2013), 117.

Even more evident is that Israel's sin with the golden calf repeats Adam's idolatry. Indeed, Richard Lints goes so far as to call the golden calf incident the paradigmatic episode of idolatry that echoes throughout the rest of the Old Testament.[5] By asking Aaron to "make us gods who shall go before us" (Exodus 32:1), Israel is violating the very first commandment of the covenant to not have any other gods before Yahweh (20:3). Like Adam before them, Israel fails in its priestly role to maintain the pure worship of Yahweh. "Rather than illuminating the created order with the reflection of YHWH, Israel now sought their significance and security from the created order."[6] They start down the path of becoming a stiff-necked people (32:9) who resemble the idol they are worshiping, acting like "rebellious cows running wild and needing to be regathered."[7] Like the golden calf, Israel is becoming "stiff-necked, hard hearted, with eyes that could not see and ears that could not hear."[8]

Just as Adam's idolatrous rebellion resulted in Yahweh confronting them, so too Israel must now face his judgment. God proposes destroying the nation for their rebellion and starting over with Moses (Exodus 32:7-10), but Moses pleads with God for mercy on the basis of God's covenant with Abraham, and God relents (32:11-14). Moses confronts the people, resulting in three thousand Israelites being killed (32:15-29). Nonetheless, God commands Moses to lead the people into the land but warns that he will not go with them (33:3). Just as Adam's sin resulted in exclusion from God's presence, now Israel's rebellious idolatry puts the promise of God's presence at risk.

Moses is distraught. Based on the favor God has already shown him, Moses pleads with God to go with the people into the land despite their sin

---

[5]Richard Lints, *Identity and Idolatry: The Image of God and Its Inversion*, NSBT 36 (Downers Grove, IL: InterVarsity Press, 2015), 89.

[6]Lints, *Identity and Idolatry*, 93.

[7]G. K. Beale, *A New Testament Biblical Theology: The Unfolding of the Old Testament in the New* (Grand Rapids, MI: Baker Books, 2011), 367. He bases this conclusion on the repetition of expressions like (1) stiff-necked (Exodus 32:9; 33:3, 5; 34:9), (2) running loose (32:25), (3) turning aside from the way (32:8), (4) gathered together again in the gate (32:26), and (5) Moses leading the people where God directed (32:34).

[8]Lints, *Identity and Idolatry*, 93-94. He further notes the repeated use of this language later in the Old Testament to describe Israel's sin (2 Chronicles 30:8; 36:13; Nehemiah 9:16-17; Job 41:24; Isaiah 6:9; 32:3; 44:18; Jeremiah 5:21; 7:26; 17:23; Ezekiel 3:7; 12:2; Psalm 95:8; 115:5-6; Zechariah 7:11).

(Exodus 33:12-13). The exchange between God and Moses that follows is stunning:

> And he said, "My presence will go with you, and I will give you rest." And he said to him, "If your presence will not go with me, do not bring us up from here. For how shall it be known that I have found favor in your sight, I and your people? Is it not in your going with us, so that we are distinct, I and your people, from every other people on the face of the earth?" (Exodus 33:14-16)[9]

Several features of this exchange stand out. First, God himself connects his presence with giving his people rest in the Promised Land. We saw a similar connection in Genesis 1–2, where God rested on the seventh day (Genesis 2:2) and then placed Adam into his garden sanctuary to enjoy his presence. Second, Moses portrays God's presence dwelling with them as a marker of Israel's status as God's people, distinguishing them from all other nations. Third, despite Israel's idolatry, God remains committed to giving his people rest in his presence. Not even persistent human rebellion can ultimately thwart God's purposes.

With this crisis averted, God renews the covenant with his people and reissues the stipulations of the covenant along with the instructions for the tabernacle, the place where his presence will dwell with his people (Exodus 34–39). Once the tabernacle is constructed (40:1-33), the glory of God's presence fills it (40:34-35). Even before Israel reaches the Promised Land, God's presence dwells with them. God has multiplied Abraham's descendants into a great nation (people). He is about to move them closer to the territory where he will dwell with them (place). God's plan to end humanity's exile away from his presence and bring the promised serpent-crusher has taken an important step forward.

WARNINGS AT THE FOOT OF SINAI

For nearly eleven months Israel remains at the foot of Mount Sinai, where Moses receives additional rules and regulations for the covenant (Leviticus 1–27; Numbers 1:1–10:10). Embedded within these covenant stipulations are a series

---

[9]Referring to Israel as a nation (*gôy*) may allude back to the use of the same word in Exodus 19:6. An additional link to this verse refers to them as holy, which connects with the description of Israel as a people distinct from others. See Blackburn, *God Who Makes Himself Known*, 174-78.

of blessings if Israel obeys (Leviticus 26:1-13) as well as curses if they disobey (26:14-39).[10] People, place, and God's presence are central to both the blessings and the curses. If Israel obeys, the land will abundantly produce crops and they will dwell securely in the land. God will multiply them and make his dwelling among them. He summarizes the culminating blessing, saying, "I will walk among you and will be your God, and you shall be my people" (26:12). Faithfulness to the covenant will lead to a near Edenic state where the promises of people, place, and God's presence will be progressively realized.[11]

People, place, and God's presence also take center stage when it comes to the curses. The land will not yield its harvest, because God will make the heavens like iron and the ground like bronze (Leviticus 26:14-20). Instead of humanity having dominion over the land, the wild beasts will kill their children and destroy their livestock (26:21-22). God will afflict the people through their enemies, eject them from the land, and scatter them among the nations (26:23-33). Instead of walking *among* his people (26:12), God will walk *against* them (26:28). While the people are in exile, the land will experience its Sabbath rest (26:34-35). Rather than multiplying and exercising dominion over the nations, God's people will perish among them away from his presence (26:36-39).

A TRAGIC REFUSAL

When the people finally set out from Mount Sinai, trouble marks their path. The Israelites have been rescued from their Egyptian bondage, but the inclination toward rebellion and idolatry remain stubbornly present. Despite Yahweh setting them apart as his firstborn son (Exodus 4:22-23) and making them a kingdom of priests (19:5-6), they are still simultaneously sons of Adam. Israel's entry into the Promised Land will be anything but smooth.

Once Israel reaches the border of the Promised Land, disaster strikes. When the people hear the scouting report from the spies, they refuse to enter the land (Numbers 13:1-14:12). Like Adam and Eve before them, the Israelites

---

[10]For a helpful categorization of the covenant blessings and curses in Leviticus and Deuteronomy, see Douglas K. Stuart, *Hosea–Jonah*, WBC 31 (Waco, TX: Word Books, 1987), xxxi-xlii.

[11]See similarly L. Michael Morales, *Who Shall Ascend the Mountain of the Lord? A Biblical Theology of the Book of Leviticus*, NSBT 37 (Downers Grove, IL: InterVarsity Press, 2015), 215-20.

decide to determine right and wrong for themselves. Instead of submitting
to Yahweh's authority and trusting his goodness and power, the kingdom of
priests follows in the footsteps of their forefathers in the garden and repeats
their failure with the golden calf. Despite the staggering promises of God's
presence going with them and the prospect of experiencing rest in the place
God had set aside for them, the people of Israel once again choose disobedience rather than faith.

The consequences are swift and disastrous. Once again Moses intercedes
to prevent God from wiping out the nation (Numbers 14:13-19). In his prayer,
Moses makes three interrelated "arguments" for why God should not make
an end of Israel. First, the Egyptians have heard that the Lord is in the midst
of his people Israel, even being seen face to face (14:13-14). Second, the nations will conclude that the Lord was unable to bring Israel into the land he
promised them (14:15-16). Third, showing steadfast love and mercy is central
to who the Lord is (14:17-19; see Exodus 34:6-7). On this basis, Moses argues,
God should not destroy Israel.

God does in fact relent from destroying the people, but their judgment is
nonetheless severe. The current generation of Israelites older than twenty
(minus Caleb and Joshua) are sentenced to wander in the wilderness for the
next forty years until they die off (Numbers 14:20-38). They will live out their
days in exile, away from the land where God had promised to dwell with
them. Their repeated sinful rebellion results in exile. Yet not all hope is lost.
The little ones they feared would become prey for the enemy will instead
inherit the land God promised. Not even the sin of his people will deter God
from fulfilling his promises and accomplishing his purposes.

WARNINGS ON THE VERGE OF ENTERING THE LAND

Deuteronomy opens as Israel's forty years of wilderness wandering comes to
an end. Moses is preparing this new generation by reminding them of what
God has already done for them through his promise to Abraham, the advancement of that promise through the exodus, and the formation of the
nation of Israel through the covenant at Sinai.

As part of their preparation for entering the Promised Land, God lays out
a series of curses that will come upon Israel if they disobey the Lord and

break his covenant, as well as blessings that will come if they obey the Lord and keep his covenant (Deuteronomy 27–30). Yet even within these chapters, Deuteronomy 28 emerges as the focal point of the blessings and curses contained within the covenant. What Leviticus 26 had articulated in seed form, Deuteronomy 28 describes in full flower. In their expanded form here in Deuteronomy 28, the focus clearly falls on curses. Woven throughout the explanation of these blessings and curses are the three key themes of people, place, and God's presence.

Blessings for obedience. Let's start with the blessings (Deuteronomy 28:1-14). If Israel obeys Yahweh by keeping his covenant, these blessings will chase them down (28:1-2) like a predator pursuing its prey. Deuteronomy 28:3-6 summarizes the basic form of the blessings. Regardless of whether the Israelites are in the city or in the fields, God's presence to bless them will be with them in the land (28:3, 6). As Israel remains faithful to the covenant stipulations, God will multiply not only their descendants but even the fruit of the ground, their livestock, and their flocks (28:4-5).

To drive home his point, Yahweh further elaborates these blessings in the section that follows (Deuteronomy 28:7-14). When enemies rise up against Israel, the Lord himself will so utterly defeat these enemies that they will flee from them in every direction (28:7). Rather than being financially or politically subject to the surrounding nations, Israel will lend to them (28:7, 12-14). As a result, "all the peoples of the earth shall see that you are called by the name of the LORD, and they shall be afraid of you" (28:10). As Israel dwells in the land, their wombs, their fields, and their livestock will be abundantly fruitful and multiply greatly (28:11-12). Their barns will be filled with crops because Yahweh will open the storehouses of heaven to give them rain and bless the work of their hands (28:12). Deuteronomy 28:11 captures well the focal point of God's blessing: "And the LORD will make you abound in prosperity, in the fruit of your womb and in the fruit of your livestock and in the fruit of your ground, within the land that the LORD swore to your fathers to give you."

By obeying the Lord, the people will live out the commission to Adam to be fruitful, multiply, and fill the land, and to rule over and subdue the land, experiencing God's presence in the land of promise. It will be Eden restored.

Curses for disobedience. Just as the blessings begin with a summary (Deuteronomy 28:1-6) followed by further elaboration (28:7-14), so too the curses are first summarized (28:15-19) and then further explained in detail (28:20-68). Like the blessings for obedience, the curses will overtake Israel no matter where they are if they break the covenant (28:15-16, 19). Rather than being abundantly fruitful, the people, the land, the livestock, and the flocks will be marked by scarcity (28:17-18). In the extended elaboration that follows (28:20-68), Moses repeatedly stresses the curses that will come if the people do not do all that is written in the law (27:26; 28:15, 45, 58). Broadly considered, these curses fall under the interrelated categories of people, place, and God's presence.

Let's begin with people. Instead of being fruitful and multiplying, they will be destroyed and perish quickly because of their sin (Deuteronomy 28:20). Various forms of disease will ravage the people, including some of the very plagues that God unleashed on the Egyptians (28:20-21, 27-29, 35). In addition to the physical suffering, the people will experience the mental and emotional hardships of confusion and frustration in all they do (28:20). They will watch others enjoy what should have been their blessings: wives, houses, vineyards, livestock, sons, and crops (28:30-31, 39-42). So desperate will be their plight that the sojourners will gain supremacy to the point of lending to the Israelites (28:43-44).

The place that God had promised to Israel will also be cursed if they break the covenant. Oppressive heat, drought, blight, and mildew will ravage the land, preventing it from producing abundance (Deuteronomy 28:22). The heavens that should pour out rain will instead turn to bronze, the ground that should be soft and fertile will instead be as hard as iron, and even the rain itself will feel like dust (28:23-24). When the people go to plant their crops, the return will be a fraction of what it should be (28:38-40).

While there is no explicit mention of God's presence (or lack thereof), it appears to lurk beneath the surface. Since the reason that Israel succeeds in battle is that Yahweh is with them to fight for them, their humiliating defeat before their enemies signals the absence of God's presence (Deuteronomy 28:25). But more prominent than the absence of God's presence is the motif of God's presence actively working *against* the people rather than *for* them. Yahweh is the active cause behind the devastation that will come on the people and the land. He sends the curses and frustration on the people (28:20-24). He causes their defeat at the hands of their enemies (28:25) and strikes them with Egyptian-like plagues (28:28-29, 35). Yahweh is the one who brings the oppressive foreign nations and leads Israel away from the land (28:36-37).

But the culminating curse is exile from the land, which combines all three elements of people, place, and presence. Yahweh himself will bring the people and their king to a foreign land where they will worship false gods (Deuteronomy 28:36). Instead of the nations being blessed by Israel, they will become "a horror, a proverb, and a byword among all the peoples where the LORD will lead you away" (28:37). Instead of growing up in the land of promise, their sons and daughters will live in captivity (28:41). This exile will be the result of Israel turning away from Yahweh in the midst of their abundance to serve other gods in utter deprivation (28:45-48). A merciless nation will devastate the land, consuming all the abundance intended for Israel to enjoy (28:49-51). They will besiege the land, bringing utter devastation; circumstances will become so desperate that the Israelites will eat their own children (28:53-57). The very plagues that Yahweh inflicted on Egypt will now be unleashed on Israel (28:58-61). Just as God took delight in multiplying them, he will now take delight in bringing them ruin (28:62-63). And the culminating curse will be God removing them from the land and scattering them among the nations, where they will languish in agony day and night (28:63-68). Instead of finding rest in the land of promise, the Lord will give them "a trembling heart and failing eyes and a languishing soul" (28:65). When future generations see this devastating judgment, they will conclude that "the anger of the LORD was kindled against this land, bringing upon it all the curses written in this book, and the LORD uprooted them from their land in anger and fury and great wrath, and cast them into another land, as they are this day" (29:27-28).

Just as in Eden, the culminating curse is exile from the land where God's presence dwells. Failure to do all that is written in the law will lead to exile, just as it did with Adam. Turning away from Yahweh through rebellion, idolatry, and covenant unfaithfulness will once again lead to exile from the place where God's presence dwells.

Before moving on, we should note that these warnings of exile are far from empty threats. They are in fact prophetic in nature, announcing in advance what will happen to Israel after Moses dies (Deuteronomy 31:29). After laying out the blessings and curses of the covenant, Moses makes it a matter of when, not if, they come to fruition (30:1). When the time comes for Moses to die, Yahweh explains that after his death the people will pursue foreign gods, break the covenant, and experience God's judgment (31:14-18). Therefore, God commands Moses to teach the people a song as a witness against the people when this happens (31:16–32:47). When Israel turns away from the Lord, God will hide his face from them (31:18). So even as the people enter the land to possess it, the ominous storm clouds of covenant unfaithfulness and judgment, culminating in exile, loom on the horizon. Yet even here judgment is not the final word, as God also holds out the promise of restoration when Israel repents (30:1-10).

ENTERING THE LAND AND A VICIOUS CYCLE

Now that God has prepared the new generation of Israelites to enter the land, Moses passes from the scene; his role in the story complete. For his failure to obey Yahweh (Numbers 20:2-13), Moses will also perish in exile. As the history of Israel unfolds in Joshua through 2 Kings, the pattern of sin leading to exile from the place of God's presence established in Genesis 1–11 once again repeats itself.[12]

At long last Israel enters the Promised Land under Joshua's leadership (Joshua 1–5). Through him God gives Israel possession of the land, progressively defeating and destroying the pagan inhabitants of the land (6:1–13:7). Yet even in the midst of their conquest, sin rears its ugly head when Achan takes spoils from the victory at Jericho that Yahweh had expressly forbidden (7:1). When Israel is subsequently defeated in battle at Ai (7:2-5), Joshua asks Yahweh why this has happened (7:7-9). Yahweh explains that Israel has broken the covenant and therefore cannot stand before their enemies until this sin

---

[12]As J. Daniel Hays notes, Joshua begins with Israel entering the land where they will experience God's presence. But in Judges, 1–2 Samuel, and 1–2 Kings, Israel repeatedly sins, which ultimately leads to their exile from the land at the close of 2 Kings. See C. Marvin Pate et al., *The Story of Israel: A Biblical Theology* (Downers Grove, IL: InterVarsity Press, 2004), 51-52.

is addressed (Joshua 7:10-12). Just as a previous generation had broken the covenant by making a golden calf, so now this generation violates the covenant by keeping for themselves objects that God had devoted to destruction. Only when Achan has been judged for his sin (Joshua 7:16-26) is Israel able to conquer Ai (8:1-29). The people then celebrate a renewal of the covenant, recalling both the blessings for obedience and the curses for disobedience that God had promised through Moses (8:30-35).

As Israel begins to experience rest in the land, this rest is not only the answer to Israel's Egyptian bondage but a fulfillment of God's covenant with Abraham, which in turn was God's plan for restoring humanity to the rest experienced in Eden itself.[13] Eventually they gain control of most of the land and divide it among the twelve tribes (Joshua 13:8–22:34). But in light of Israel's track record to this point, Joshua not only reminds the people of what God has done for them (23:1–24:13) but calls them to put away their foreign gods and devote themselves wholly to the Lord (24:14-28). Despite Israel's confident assertion that they will serve the Lord (24:16-18), Joshua does not share their confidence (24:19-24). He warns the people that if they break the covenant by serving other gods, "you shall perish quickly from off the good land that he has given to you" (Joshua 23:16).

That is exactly what happens after Joshua and the elders of his generation die off. The book of Judges opens with a sobering list of the peoples that Israel failed to drive out of the land (Judges 1:27-36). Yet behind Israel's failure is the sovereign purpose of God, who left these nations to test Israel (3:1). From that point forward a recurring pattern begins: (1) Israel rebels against the Lord by pursuing other gods; (2) the Lord raises up enemies to plunder and oppress Israel; (3) Israel cries out for deliverance; (4) the Lord raises up a judge (not in our modern sense of a legal official who decides cases, but a military leader) to rescue Israel from their enemies; (5) the judge delivers Israel from their enemies; (6) Israel experiences rest in the land.

For the next four centuries this pattern repeats itself, but over time the rebellion increases while the extent of the deliverance and the period of rest both decrease. For example, when the first judge, Othniel, delivers Israel, the

---

[13]Pate et al., *Story of Israel*, 53-54.

people and the land experience forty years of rest (Judges 3:7-12). But by the time of Samson—the final judge mentioned in the book—Israel is not even delivered from their enemies; there is no mention of rest for either Israel or the land (13:1–16:31).

Even though Israel physically remains in the land during these periods of subjection to their enemies, they are in fact experiencing a form of exile. What makes the land special is not its geography but the God who dwells with them there. As we have seen, the Bible consistently connects rest and God's presence with his people in the land (Genesis 2:2; Exodus 33:14; Joshua 1:13-15). So even when Israel is physically in the land, they can still experience a form of spiritual exile because of their idolatry. Along with this spiritual exile there is evidence that other covenant curses are being poured out on Israel. The book of Judges frames the repeated cycle of judgment for Israel's covenant unfaithfulness as an expression of Yahweh's anger, resulting in him opposing Israel in battle (Judges 2:11-15; Leviticus 26:17). They must pay tribute to their oppressors (Judges 3:18). The crops the Israelites plant are consumed by their enemies (Judges 6:3-6; Deuteronomy 28:30-33), which likely led to some form of famine (Leviticus 26:26). Israel's oppressors force them to worship other gods (Judges 6:25-32; Deuteronomy 28:36, 64). While these curses have not reached their full consummation, Israel experiences them in an inaugurated form even as they remain in the land.

This observation that it is possible to experience a form of exile while still living in the land will prove valuable as the biblical story line unfolds. Exile is much more than simply being physically away from the Garden of Eden or the Promised Land. What God's people need most is to experience his presence, but simply being in the land does not guarantee they will do so. Yet as we will also see, God's people can still experience his presence even when they are not in the place (the garden, the land, the new creation) he sets apart for them.

A KINGDOM AND ITS SPLIT

After limping through centuries of intermittent leadership from the judges, Israel eventually asks for a king (1 Samuel 8). On paper, Saul has all the necessary qualifications—size, looks, and wealth (9:1-2). Despite a good start to his reign, the Lord rejects Saul as king because he disobeys (1 Samuel 15). In his place God anoints David (1 Samuel 16), who despite winning numerous battles for Saul spends a number of years on the run from him. Despite being the rightful king, David lives in exile as he hides in and out of the land of Israel.

When Saul finally dies and David assumes the throne, God's promises of people, place, and presence begin to be more fully realized. In response to David's desire to build Yahweh a house (i.e., a temple for God's presence to dwell in), Yahweh promises to build David a house (i.e., a dynasty of kings). This promise is so important to the biblical story line that we need to take a closer look:

> Thus says the LORD of hosts, I took you from the pasture, from following the sheep, that you should be prince over my people Israel. And I have been with you wherever you went and have cut off all your enemies from before you. And I will make for you a great name, like the name of the great ones of the earth. And I will appoint a place for my people Israel and will plant them, so that they may dwell in their own place and be disturbed no more. And violent men shall afflict them no more, as formerly, from the time that I appointed judges over my people Israel. And I will give you rest from all your enemies. Moreover, the LORD declares to you that the LORD will make you a house. When your days are fulfilled and you lie down with your fathers, I will raise up your offspring after you, who shall come from your body, and I will establish his kingdom. He shall build a house for my name, and I will establish the throne of his kingdom forever. . . . And your house and your kingdom shall be made sure forever before me. Your throne shall be established forever. (2 Samuel 7:8-13, 16)

What God promises David is in essence a development and expansion of the promise made to Abraham.[14] As a king from Abraham's line, David inherits the promises of people and place. God will plant his people in the land, where they will live in peace and have rest from their enemies. God's presence will dwell with them. From the line of David will come a king who will build a house for Yahweh and rule over an eternal kingdom. When fully realized, it

---

[14]For a helpful discussion of 2 Samuel 7 including connections back to Genesis 1–2, see Peter J. Gentry and Stephen J. Wellum, *Kingdom Through Covenant: A Biblical-Theological Understanding of the Covenants* (Wheaton, IL: Crossway, 2012), 392-401.

will be nothing less than Eden restored, with an obedient king exercising authority over a land where God dwells with his people.

God's promise to David finds initial and partial fulfillment in his son Solomon, who builds a temple where God's presence dwells (1 Kings 6–8). His reign is the high point of Israel's history, marked by Israel's territory expanding and the nation living at peace with her neighbors. It is the closest that Israel ever comes to realizing the promise of living in a new Eden under an Adamic king and being a blessing to the nations.[15] Yet a careful look at 1 Kings 1–11 reveals cracks in Solomon's character, as he violates the stipulations for kings (Deuteronomy 17:14-20) by marrying foreign wives, accumulating horses and chariots from Egypt, and amassing large quantities of gold and silver.[16]

Eventually these cracks break through the façade of the semi-Edenic state of Solomon's reign. His large number of foreign wives who worshiped foreign gods drew him away from the Lord, and as a result God split the nation of Israel into two distinct kingdoms upon Solomon's death. Ten tribes formed the Northern Kingdom of Israel, while the tribes of Judah and Benjamin formed the Southern Kingdom of Judah. To cement the split from Judah, Israel anoints their own king, named Jeroboam, who creates two sanctuaries with golden calves as worship centers to prevent his people from going to Jerusalem to worship. Over the next two centuries, Israel spirals downward into increasing levels of idolatry. The result of their covenant unfaithfulness is exile at the hands of the Assyrians, who conquer Israel in 722 BC and take a significant portion of the population back to Assyria.

Judah, despite living under the rule of Davidic kings, fares only slightly better. Their decline into idolatry and covenant unfaithfulness is more gradual and punctuated with occasional seasons of renewal under kings who were faithful to Yahweh. But ultimately they too reach a point where their rebellion against Yahweh is so great that God brings judgment in the form of the Babylonians. In three successive waves, the Babylonians conquer Judah and bring exiles back with them to Babylon. The final conquest in 586 BC is especially devastating, as the Babylonians destroy the temple and leave only

---

[15]See similarly Dempster, *Dominion and Dynasty*, 147-48.
[16]Helpfully noted by Hays in Pate et al., *Story of Israel*, 64-65.

the poorest of the land behind to eke out a meager existence. All but lost seem the promises of a king from the lines of Abraham and David who will obey where Adam failed and rule over God's people in righteousness in a land where God's presence dwells.

We will take a closer look at how both Israel and Judah were sent into exile in the next chapter. But now we need to explore the repeated warnings about exile that God gave his people throughout their history, leading up to their eventual judgment.

WARNINGS WHILE LIVING IN THE LAND

Despite the persistent unfaithfulness of both Israel and Judah, God refused to let his people rush headlong toward judgment without repeated warnings about the wrath to come. Yahweh raised up prophets to call the people to repent from their idolatry and covenant unfaithfulness and to turn back to the Lord. Although we cannot look at all the relevant passages, we can explore a few from different points in the history of Israel and Judah as a series of snapshots that show God's repeated warnings about the coming judgment.

Hosea ministered to both the Northern and Southern Kingdoms during the eighth century BC. Despite experiencing significant prosperity, Israel was spiritually bankrupt and sprinting headfirst toward God's judgment. Because they broke Yahweh's covenant, they are about to reap the consequences of God's judgment in the form of the Assyrians (Hosea 8:1-10). Not even their ritual performance of the Mosaic law covenant will save them (8:11-13). Yahweh "will remember their iniquity and punish their sins; they shall return to Egypt" (8:13) because Israel has forgotten her maker (8:14).[17]

Because Israel has played the whore by going after other gods, the land will not yield its harvest (Hosea 9:1-2). But the culminating form of judgment is exile: "They shall not remain in the land of the LORD, but Ephraim shall return to Egypt, and they shall eat unclean food in Assyria" (9:3). As a result, they will no longer be able to offer their sacrifices and observe the festivals (9:4-6). God's judgment of exile is coming because of Israel's rejection of the

---

[17]Since the context clearly has in view Israel's captivity in Assyria, Egypt is used symbolically to refer to a place of captivity outside the land. Because Israel has broken the covenant, they are in effect returning to the land where they lived before the covenant was cut.

prophets (9:7-9), their pursuit of Baal (9:10-14), and their syncretistic religious practices (9:15-17). Israel's prosperity has led them away from fearing the Lord to trusting in their idolatrous golden calf (10:1-6). The line of kings will come to an end, the land will become overgrown, and Israel will be completely overrun by her enemies (10:7-15).

Throughout this section, the themes of people, place, and presence are interwoven to show the comprehensive nature of Yahweh's judgment on Israel. The people that were supposed to be fruitful and multiply will become few in number. The king, who was supposed to defeat their enemies and secure peace for the people, will be led off in chains. The place that was supposed to resemble a new Eden will instead be overrun with thorn and thistle. Instead of experiencing God's presence in the land, Israel will follow their idolatrous golden calf into captivity in Assyria. Just as Adam and Eve were exiled from Eden for their sinful rebellion, so too Israel will be sent away from the land for their covenant unfaithfulness.

The beginning of Isaiah's ministry overlapped with Hosea, but Isaiah's focus was on the Southern Kingdom of Judah. Judah's eventual exile from the land for their covenant unfaithfulness is a central theme in the book. While the dark clouds of exile loom on the horizon throughout Isaiah (e.g., 1:2-31; 2:6–4:1; 5:14, 29-30), these threats appear to be coming to fruition when the Assyrians invade Judah in 701 BC (Isaiah 36:1-22). But Judah is granted a reprieve when King Hezekiah prays for God to show them mercy. Yahweh responds by striking 185,000 Assyrians dead and sending their king back to their homeland, where he is murdered by his own sons (37:1-38). Crisis averted, right?

Wrong. It was merely crisis delayed. Shortly after the Assyrians leave, Hezekiah becomes deathly ill but has his life spared by Yahweh (Isaiah 38:1-21). The king of Babylon sends envoys with a gift for Hezekiah, and he gives them the grand tour of his treasure house (39:1-4). When Isaiah hears of this, the prophet announces God's judgment (39:6-7). As far as God is concerned, exile in Babylon is a settled matter. All that the Davidic kings had worked to accumulate will be taken away to fill the treasuries of Babylon. Worse yet, his descendants, members of the line of promise through whom the serpent-crusher will come, will be taken away into exile and become eunuchs unable to continue the line of promise. Rather than ruling over the land of promise, they will dwell as servants in the land of judgment.

When God calls Jeremiah to be his spokesman nearly seventy-five years later, Judah's situation is even worse. Not even the reforms of the godly King Josiah (640–609 BC) are able to turn the tide of God's judgment (2 Kings 22:1–23:30). During the years leading up to exile, Jeremiah repeatedly warns the people of the coming judgment. As an enacted parable about his sovereignty, God sends Jeremiah to a potter's house (Jeremiah 18:1-6). Because he is the potter, Yahweh has the authority to "pluck up and break down and destroy" any nation that rebels against him as well as to turn away from that judgment if that nation repents (18:7-10). From this general statement, Yahweh turns to a direct warning against Judah: "Behold, I am shaping disaster against you and devising a plan against you. Return, every one from his evil way, and amend your ways and your deeds" (18:11).

But when Judah doubles down on their stubborn rebellion (Jeremiah 18:12), the Lord announces judgment. He marvels that Judah has forgotten him and has instead pursued false gods that lead them away from the path of righteousness (18:13-15). As a result, the land of promise has become "a horror, a thing to be hissed at forever. Everyone who passes by it is horrified and shakes his head" (18:16). Instead of a new Eden that nations would marvel at, the land will become a symbol of utter destruction that makes the nations derisively hiss. Yahweh vows that "like the east wind I will scatter them before the enemy" (18:17). This means more than simple defeat in battle, as the verb *scatter* (Heb. *pûṣ*) regularly refers to God sending his people into exile (see Deuteronomy 28:64; Jeremiah 9:16; 13:24; 30:11; 40:15; Ezekiel 11:16). Instead of Judah experiencing God's presence, Yahweh asserts "I will show them my back, not my face, in the day of their calamity" (Jeremiah 18:17). Judah's persistent idolatry, rebellion, and covenant unfaithfulness will lead to their exile from the land. God's people will be cut off from his property and presence.

Among the second wave of exiles in 597 BC was a young priest named Ezekiel whom God called as his prophet in 592 BC (Ezekiel 1:1-5). God reveals to him in a vision the stunning idolatry taking place in the Jerusalem temple, which leads to the glory of the Lord leaving the temple (8:1–11:25).

With God's presence now gone from the land, God commands Ezekiel to give the people a picture of exile. Ezekiel is instructed to take "an exile's baggage, and go into exile by day in their sight" (Ezekiel 12:1-7). The Lord tells Ezekiel to explain his actions to the people. After stating that the king and the people of Judah will go into exile (12:8-13), Yahweh says:

> And I will scatter toward every wind all who are around him, his helpers and all his troops, and I will unsheathe the sword after them. And they shall know that I am the LORD, when I disperse them among the nations and scatter them among the countries. But I will let a few of them escape from the sword, from famine and pestilence, that they may declare all their abominations among the nations where they go, and may know that I am the LORD. (Ezekiel 12:14-16)

Instead of being fruitful and multiplying in the land, only a few will be left, and they will be scattered among the nations. Instead of being rooted in a land resembling a new Eden, they will be strangers in foreign lands, forced to endure famine and pestilence. Instead of God dwelling with his people, he will no longer be with them. And the ultimate purpose behind this judgment is that those who are in exile will know that Yahweh is the one true God.

CONCLUSION AND APPLICATION

These warnings are just a sample of countless more that God spoke through his prophets. Yahweh repeatedly makes it clear that exile means far more than simply being removed from the land. It is the culminating judgment for repeated rebellion and idolatry. As such, it is a physical representation of an even greater spiritual reality—separation from the living God. Like Adam and Eve before them, Israel and Judah's sin led to separation from a holy God. The very people God set apart to be fruitful and multiply in the land resembling a new Eden would instead be left few in number, scattered among the nations, and separated from the place where God dwells. When that exile finally came because of Israel and Judah's persistent idolatry and rebellion, no one should have been surprised. Yet the devastation that exile brought with it was nonetheless staggering. In the next chapter we will look at just how bad it was.

But before we move on, take a moment to consider the incredible patience that the Lord shows to his people. As the Bible rapidly marches through Israel's history, we can lose sight of the hundreds of years that pass as God repeatedly pleads with his people to repent. If we are honest, we too can point to specific areas in our lives where God has patiently endured our persistent sin. The apostle Paul explains that God's patience and kindness toward us in our sin is intended to lead us to turn away from it (Romans 2:4). Perhaps nowhere is God's patience toward sinners displayed more clearly than on the cross, where God in the flesh endured the ignorant and sinful taunts of those around him (Matthew 27:39-44). Even more stunningly, Jesus asked the Father to forgive them (Luke 23:34). Take a moment right now to marvel at God's patience toward you; after all, "because of the LORD's faithful love we do not perish, for his mercies never end" (Lamentations 3:22 CSB).

Chapter Three

THE REALITY OF EXILE
WHEN ISRAEL REBELLED

SOMETIMES THE DREAD of an undesirable event is worse than the event itself. Such was not the case with exile. Every awful aspect of exile the prophets warned about came to pass, and then some. Despite God's repeated warnings through his covenant lawyers the prophets, both Israel and Judah stubbornly continued to be stiff-necked people, following in the footsteps of their ancestors who made the golden calf at the foot of Sinai. Just as Adam and Eve were exiled from the garden for their idolatry and rebellion, so now Israel is sent out from the Promised Land for violating the covenant through their worship of false gods.

The threats we explored in the previous chapter made it clear that God was not kidding around about the seriousness of his people's sin. In this chapter, we will now see these threats come to their full and devastating fruition. To capture the full scope of the exile, we will look at it in three stages. We will first look at the exile of the Northern Kingdom of Israel and then at the exile of the Southern Kingdom of Judah. Finally, we will look at different snapshots of life during the exile. Along the way we will see why

Same with the 'exile' from Eden?

exile was such a defining experience for God's people that it left an enduring mark on their identity.

THE FALL OF THE NORTHERN KINGDOM

By the time that 722 BC came along, Israel could no longer maneuver and manipulate its way out of the impending Assyrian doom. The pragmatic placing of golden calves as worship centers by their first king, Jeroboam, set a trajectory of idolatry that led to Israel's downfall. God's instrument of judgment was the Assyrians, who after a three-year siege carried many of the Israelites off to various cities in the Assyrian Empire (2 Kings 17:6).

In the section that follows (2 Kings 17:7-18), the author makes it crystal clear that sin was the root cause of their exile. The fundamental category of Israel's sin is covenant unfaithfulness. They sinned against Yahweh, the one who brought them out of slavery in Egypt. Like their fathers—who broke the covenant less than two months after God appeared to them in smoke and fire on Sinai—they stubbornly failed to trust the Lord. Israel was not merely indifferent to the commandments and statutes of the covenant; they despised them! Even with the repeated warnings of the prophets, Israel remained steadfast in their commitment to evil. *(unlike Raiders under Al Davis)*

But by far the most consistent and persistent expression of unfaithfulness to the covenant was Israel's idolatry. Look again at how many different times it is mentioned, whether directly or implicitly in 2 Kings 17, Israel

- feared others gods (v. 7)
- walked in the customs of the nations the Lord drove out (v. 8)
- walked in the customs the kings of Israel practiced (v. 8)
- built high places in all their towns (v. 9)
- built pillars and Asherim, making offerings on all the high places, just like the nations before them (vv. 10-11)
- served idols (v. 12)
- went after false idols and became false (v. 15)
- followed the surrounding nations (v. 15)
- made metal images of two golden calves (v. 16; cf. 17:21-23)

- made an Asherah (v. 16)
- worshiped all the host of heaven (v. 16)
- served Baal (v. 16)
- burned their sons and daughters as offerings (v. 17)
- used divination and omens (v. 17)

As if this list were not impressive enough, the author roots Israel's problems in a fatal mistake they made when the kingdom split—they walked in the sins of Jeroboam, the first king of the Northern Kingdom (2 Kings 17:21-23). As we noted in the previous chapter, Jeroboam built golden calves and placed them in the cities of Dan and Bethel to prevent his people from traveling to Jerusalem to worship there (1 Kings 12:25-33). Idolatry was the foundation of Israel's covenant unfaithfulness, and just as God had warned (Deuteronomy 28:58-68), exile from the land was the inevitable consequence.

THE FALL OF JUDAH

The Southern Kingdom of Judah lasted barely a century more before a similar fate befell them. Not even the substantial reforms led by Josiah—the best king since David and Solomon (2 Kings 23:25)—were able to turn away the storm cloud of God's wrath from Judah. Exile crashed on Judah in three different tidal waves, leaving in their wake destruction and devastation.

The first wave (605 BC). The first wave landed in 605 BC. After paying tribute to King Nebuchadnezzar of Babylon for three years, King Jehoiakim rebelled. In response, Nebuchadnezzar sent his armies to punish Judah. But far more than a simple geopolitical conflict was taking place:

> According to the word of the LORD that he spoke by his servants the prophets. Surely this came upon Judah at the command of the LORD, to remove them out of his sight, for the sins of Manasseh, according to all that he had done, and also for the innocent blood that he had shed. For he filled Jerusalem with innocent blood, and the LORD would not pardon. (2 Kings 24:2-4)

God was fulfilling his repeated promises of judgment, issued through numerous prophets (most recently Jeremiah). Behind the rage of a Babylonian king was the sovereign purpose of Yahweh, raising up foreign, pagan kings to further his purposes. And what was that purpose? To remove Judah from the land he had given them.

Once again, sin is the reason for Judah's exile. In particular, the "sins of Manasseh" are singled out. Despite being the son of the godly King Hezekiah, Manasseh plunged the nation headlong into idolatry. During his fifty-five-year reign, Manasseh not only overturned every reform his father had instituted but surpassed the idolatry of any of his predecessors. According to 2 Kings 21:2-9, Manasseh

- followed the practices of the nations God drove out of the land (v. 2)
- rebuilt the high places his father Hezekiah had torn down (v. 3)
- built altars for Baal and made an Asherah just like King Ahab of Israel (v. 3)
- worshiped and served the whole host of heaven (v. 3)
- built altars for the host of heaven in the temple courts of the Lord's house (vv. 4-5)
- burned his own son as an offering (v. 6)
- consulted fortune-tellers, mediums, necromancers, and omens (v. 6)
- placed an Asherah in the house of the Lord (v. 7)

In light of this litany of his covenant unfaithfulness, the author states that "Manasseh led [Judah] astray to do more evil than the nations had done whom the LORD destroyed before the people of Israel" (2 Kings 21:9). On top of all that, "Manasseh shed very much innocent blood, till he had filled Jerusalem from one end to another" (21:16). Just as Jeroboam had become the paradigmatic king for Israel's idolatry and covenant rebellion, Manasseh stood out as the king who most clearly defined Judah's descent toward destruction.

Daniel 1:1-4 describes the aftermath of Nebuchadnezzar's conquest. In addition to taking vessels from the temple in Jerusalem and placing them in the treasury of his own god, he took the best and the brightest young men to indoctrinate them in the literature and language of the Chaldeans. Among those men were Daniel and his friends Hananiah, Mishael, and Azariah (better known as Shadrach, Meshach, and Abednego).

Second wave (597 BC). Meanwhile, back in Judah, circumstances continued to deteriorate. Instead of being chastened by their humiliation at the hands of the Babylonians, Judah's leadership doubled down on its sinful ways. Initially there seemed to be hopeful signs, as King Jehoiakim turned to Egypt for help. Despite God's warning that Egypt would not be able to prevent Babylon from conquering Jerusalem (Jeremiah 46:1-26), Jehoiakim aligned himself with Egypt and eventually paid the price. He died with the Babylonians on his doorstep, and a mere three months into the reign of his son Jehoiachin, Nebuchadnezzar besieged Jerusalem (2 Kings 24:8-17). Seeing the writing on the wall, Jehoiachin surrendered to the Babylonians. In addition to taking treasures from the king's house and the temple, Nebuchadnezzar took into captivity "all the officials and all the mighty men of valor, 10,000 captives, and all the craftsmen and the smiths. None remained, except the poorest people of the land" (2 Kings 24:14). Nebuchadnezzar appointed Jehoiachin's uncle Mattaniah in his place, renaming him Zedekiah (2 Kings 24:17). Among this second wave of exiles was a young priest named Ezekiel (Ezekiel 1:1-3), who would be God's spokesman to his captive people in Babylon for at least two decades.

Third wave (586 BC). Despite the devastation of the first two waves, Judah continued down the path of destruction. Zedekiah followed in the evil footsteps of his predecessors, and finally God had had enough: "For because of the anger of the LORD it came to the point in Jerusalem and Judah that he cast them out from his presence" (2 Kings 24:20). The time for the cup of Yahweh's wrath to be poured out had come (Jeremiah 25:15-36).

So Zedekiah rebels against the Babylonians, and this time Nebuchadnezzar was fed up. After a two-year siege, the Babylonians capture a fleeing Zedekiah. The last thing he sees before they gouge out his eyes is the execution of his sons. He is led off to Babylon in chains, along with the leaders of the people, leaving only the poorest of the land behind (2 Kings 25:11-12). To minimize the risk of future rebellion, the Babylonians broke down the city walls and burned down the temple, the king's houses, and every great house in the entire city (25:8-10). Every remaining bit of valuable metal from the temple was taken back to Babylon (24:13-17). Jerusalem lay in tatters, just as God had promised.

Lest the reader think Jerusalem's destruction was merely a geopolitical event brought about by a lack of diplomatic savvy from the kings of Judah, 2 Chronicles 36:12-16 makes it clear this was the Lord's doing. Zedekiah was a stiff-necked, hard-hearted king who did evil in the sight of Yahweh by failing to humble himself before the prophet Jeremiah and rebelling against Nebuchadnezzar (36:12-13). The root cause of Judah's exile was their unfaithfulness to the covenant God had made with them. And the primary manifestation of that rebellion against Yahweh was "following all the abominations of the nations" (36:14); in other words, worshiping other so-called gods and engaging in the wicked practices associated with their idolatry. They continued to do this for generations despite the repeated warnings from prophets like Jeremiah (36:15-16). Like their forefathers, they proved to be stiff-necked and hardhearted.

Several verses later we gain further insight into the Lord's purpose when the chronicler asserts that the destruction of Jerusalem and the ensuing exile happened "to fulfill the word of the LORD by the mouth of Jeremiah, until the land had enjoyed its Sabbaths. All the days that it lay desolate it kept Sabbath, to fulfill seventy years" (2 Chronicles 36:21). Nearly eighteen years before these tragic events, Jeremiah had announced this would happen (Jeremiah 25:1-14). But the most striking wrinkle is that the people would remain in exile until the land could enjoy its Sabbaths, which is exactly what Leviticus 26:34-35 had foretold centuries before. The Sabbath was a sign of the covenant that God made with his people. It was intended to remind God's people of their dependence on him by giving them a day of rest and refreshment dedicated to worshiping the Lord. But it was also intended to provide rest to the land, and because of the people's covenant unfaithfulness the land did not experience the rest it needed. Now God is sending his people into exile to purify the land in anticipation of the return of a purified remnant.

With Jerusalem devastated, the temple in ruins, the king dead, and most of the people in exile, God's promise to Abraham of people, place, and presence seems on the verge of collapse.[1] The words of Lamentations 1:1-3 capture the emotional state of the people in the aftermath:

---

[1]For an attempt to summarize and survey the historical and sociological impact of the exile, see D. L. Smith-Christopher, "Reassessing the Historical and Sociological Impact of the Babylonian

How lonely sits the city
  that was full of people!
How like a widow has she become,
  she who was great among the nations!
She who was a princess among the provinces
  has become a slave.
She weeps bitterly in the night,
  with tears on her cheeks;
among all her lovers
  she has none to comfort her;
all her friends have dealt treacherously with her;
  they have become her enemies.
Judah has gone into exile because of affliction
  and hard servitude;
she dwells now among the nations,
  but finds no resting place;
her pursuers have all overtaken her
  in the midst of her distress.

So how would God's people persevere in the midst of such despair?[2]

LIFE IN EXILE

In the aftermath of Jerusalem's destruction, God's people were forced to pick up the pieces and make the best of seemingly being abandoned by him.[3] Although Scripture does not give us a significant amount of detail regarding what life in exile was like, there are enough passages to sketch a general portrait. Despite knowing what was coming, Jeremiah was grief-stricken when God's wrath was poured out on Jerusalem. With the city and temple

---

Exile (597/587–539 BCE)," in *Exile: Old Testament, Jewish, and Christian Conceptions*, ed. James M. Scott (Leiden, The Netherlands: Brill, 1997), 7-36.

[2]Dempster observes that 2 Chronicles being the final book of the Hebrew canon signals that "*Israel is still in exile even though it has returned.*" Stephen G. Dempster, *Dominion and Dynasty: A Biblical Theology of the Hebrew Bible*, NSBT 15 (Downers Grove, IL: InterVarsity Press, 2003), 224, emphasis original.

[3]For a concise description of life in exile and its consequences, see John Goldingay, *Old Testament Theology*, vol. 1, *Israel's Gospel* (Downers Grove, IL: InterVarsity Press, 2003), 698-707.

in ruins, the prophet wrote what we refer to as the book of Lamentations.
Just listen to his sorrow:

> My eyes are spent with weeping;
>> my stomach churns;
> my bile is poured out to the ground
>> because of the destruction of the daughter of my people,
> because infants and babies faint
>> in the streets of the city.
> They cry to their mothers,
>> "Where is bread and wine?"
> as they faint like a wounded man
>> in the streets of the city,
> as their life is poured out
>> on their mothers' bosom.
> What can I say for you, to what compare you,
>> O daughter of Jerusalem?
> What can I liken to you, that I may comfort you,
>> O virgin daughter of Zion?
> For your ruin is vast as the sea;
>> who can heal you? (Lamentations 2:11-13)

Even though Jeremiah knows that God has promised to bring back a
remnant and fulfill his promises through a new covenant (Jeremiah 31:31-34),
the prophet concludes the book by praying for God to restore his people
"unless you have utterly rejected us, and you remain exceedingly angry with
us" (Lamentations 5:21-22). Even knowing the promises of restoration, Jeremiah wonders aloud whether Yahweh is done with the Jewish people for good.

We see a similar note of grief and sorrow in Psalm 137, which was written
by one of the exiles while in Babylon:

> By the waters of Babylon,
>> there we sat down and wept,
>> when we remembered Zion.
> On the willows there
>> we hung up our lyres.

For there our captors
  required of us songs,
and our tormentors, mirth, saying,
    "Sing us one of the songs of Zion!". . .
O daughter of Babylon, doomed to be destroyed,
    blessed shall he be who repays you
    with what you have done to us!
Blessed shall he be who takes your little ones
    and dashes them against the rock! (Psalm 137:1-2, 8-9)

The pain and anguish are palpable, the grief indescribable, the thirst for vengeance understandable. Everything that seemed foundational to their identity has been destroyed.

In the midst of this sorrow, frustration, and longing for their homeland, the exiles faced two fundamental challenges: (1) remaining faithful to Yahweh in a land full of idolatry and (2) trusting that Yahweh would sovereignly work out his plans to fulfill his promises. Let's take a look at God's message to his people in the midst of these daunting realities.[4]

Remaining faithful to Yahweh. As noted above, when the first wave of exiles arrived in Babylon in 605 BC, Nebuchadnezzar commanded his chief eunuch to find the best and the brightest among the Jews to serve in his administration. As a result, Daniel, Shadrach, Meschach, and Abednego were selected for various positions, with Daniel serving for the entire time of the exile. Throughout their service in the royal administration, they were repeatedly confronted with the worship of other gods.

When Nebuchadnezzar makes a ninety-foot-high golden image and requires everyone to bow down in worship before it, Shadrach, Meshach, and Abednego refuse. Even when Nebuchadnezzar threatens to throw them into a fiery furnace, these faithful Jewish men express their faith in God's power to deliver them (Daniel 3:17). But even if God should choose not to deliver them, they boldly say, "Be it known to you, O king, that we will not serve

---

[4]One issue that cannot be dealt with here is the role of the exile in the formation of the Hebrew canon. See, e.g., James Sanders, "The Exile and Canon Formation," in *Exile: Old Testament, Jewish, and Christian Conceptions*, ed. James M. Scott (Leiden, The Netherlands: Brill, 1997), 37-61.

your gods or worship the golden image that you have set up" (3:18). When God miraculously delivers them from the flames of the furnace, even Nebuchadnezzar is forced to admit there is no God like Yahweh, going so far as to prohibit anyone from speaking against him (3:28-30). Although Daniel appears to have avoided this particular crisis (the text does not say how or why), he is faced with his own many years later under King Darius of Persia. When Daniel refuses to obey an injunction against praying to any other god besides the king, he is thrown into a den of lions overnight (6:1-18). Yahweh honors Daniel's trust in him by preserving his life (6:19-24), and King Darius is so moved that he issues a decree that everyone in his kingdom should "tremble and fear before the God of Daniel" because Yahweh has an everlasting kingdom (6:25-28).

In the book of Ezekiel, we glimpse life in exile from a different perspective yet see the same issue of idolatry. Serving as God's prophet to the exiles in Babylon, Ezekiel repeatedly rebukes and condemns their idolatry. Ezekiel 14 records a time when the elders of Israel came to the prophet to consult the Lord. What they get is a blistering rebuke for their ongoing idolatry. These elders "have taken their idols into their hearts, and set the stumbling block of their iniquity before their faces" (Ezekiel 14:3) and therefore "are estranged from me through their idols" (14:5). For those who refuse the call to repent from their idolatry, the Lord says, "I will set my face against that man; I will make him a sign and a byword and cut him off from the midst of my people, and you shall know that I am the LORD" (14:8). The purpose of this punishment is "that the house of Israel may no more go astray from me, nor defile themselves anymore with all their transgressions, but that they may be my people and I may be their God, declares the Lord GOD" (14:11). Not even removal from the land was enough to uproot the idols from the hearts of the elders.

Trusting Yahweh to fulfill his promises. In the midst of exile, God reassures his people that he remains sovereign and will work out his plans for his people. In fact, some of God's most comforting oracles originate during what on the surface appears to be the darkest hour for God's people. As a result, God's stunning promises of a new covenant (e.g., Jeremiah 31:31-34; Ezekiel 36:22-38) shine all the brighter, as we shall see in the next chapter. But in this section we will look at three examples that stress God's commitment to sovereignly work out his purposes, one each from Daniel, Esther, and Jeremiah.

Over the course of his seventy-plus years in Babylon, Daniel has repeated visions and dreams focused on this truth. Just a few years after arriving in Babylon, Daniel interprets a dream of King Nebuchadnezzar that portrays a series of kingdoms ruling over the region (Daniel 2:31-45). That vision culminates in an eternal kingdom established by God that will crush all other kingdoms (2:44-45). Nearly fifty years later, Daniel has another vision. This time he sees "one like a son of man" who approaches the "Ancient of Days" and receives an eternal kingdom over "all peoples, nations, and languages" that he shares with "the people of the saints of the Most High" (7:1-28). Shortly after the Persians conquer the Babylonians in 539 BC, Daniel has another series of visions. Recognizing that the end of the seventy years of exile was drawing to a close, Daniel prays a long prayer, confessing the people's history of rebellion and asking God to show mercy in bringing an end to their exile (9:3-19). In response, God sends the angel Gabriel with a message for Daniel: seventy weeks (of years) have been decreed to accomplish God's purposes for his people, during which an anointed one will be cut off (9:24-27). That same year God gave Daniel another vision further detailing the outworking of God's purposes for his people and his kingdom, culminating in the resurrection of God's people to everlasting life (11:1–12:13). These visions make it clear that God's saving purposes go beyond Israel to address humanity's exile from God's presence and his commitment to fulfill his intention for creation expressed in Genesis 1-2.

Although the book of Daniel never indicates he passed these visions on to the people, it seems probable that Daniel did. These prophetic visions and dreams would have served to fuel the faith of the exiles struggling to remain faithful to Yahweh. The challenge would be trusting the Lord to fulfill his promises despite the hardships of exile in a pagan land.

The book of Esther presents a similar reality.[5] Through a remarkable series of events, a Jewish woman named Esther becomes queen to King Ahasuerus

---

[5]Lee Beach, *The Church in Exile: Living in Hope After Christendom* (Downers Grove, IL: InterVarsity Press, 2015), 69-80, describes Esther as a book of advice for exiles, with particular emphasis on trusting God's sovereign plan and living a life holiness.

of Persia in the early fifth century BC (Esther 1–2). When Haman, an advisor to the king, crafts a plot to destroy the Jews (Esther 3), Esther and her uncle Mordecai work together to thwart this plan and preserve the Jewish people (Esther 4–10). Although the name of God is never specifically mentioned in the book, it is apparent that he is the one working in and through the actions of the various characters to both protect his people and advance his purposes.

We see the same emphasis from a different angle in Jeremiah. Shortly after the second wave of exiles was sent off to Babylon, Jeremiah wrote them a letter instructing them what to do. In contrast to the false prophets claiming that exile would not last very long, Jeremiah exhorts the exiles:

> Build houses and live in them; plant gardens and eat their produce. Take wives and have sons and daughters; take wives for your sons, and give your daughters in marriage, that they may bear sons and daughters; multiply there, and do not decrease. But seek the welfare of the city where I have sent you into exile, and pray to the LORD on its behalf, for in its welfare you will find your welfare. (Jeremiah 29:5-7)

God had already told Jeremiah that the exile would last seventy years (Jeremiah 25:11-13); here, he instructs the people to settle into the normal routines of life. But God reiterates his promise to restore them from exile after seventy years, gathering them back to the land (29:10-14). The challenge facing the exiles is whether they will trust in God to fulfill his promises. Given the hardships of exile, it would be easy to conclude that God was done with Judah. Things only got worse when the Babylonians destroyed the temple. Would these exiles cling to God's promises in the face of seemingly insurmountable circumstances?

As a result of the exile, the Jewish people began to spread out beyond Babylon throughout the Mediterranean world. In the centuries that followed, sizable Jewish populations sprung up in many of the largest cities. This dispersion of Jewish people came to be known as the Diaspora, a term that the New Testament picks up at several points (John 7:35; James 1:1; 1 Peter 1:1-2). This Diaspora helped set the stage for the spread of the gospel, as the apostle Paul would use the synagogues in the Diaspora as the launching point for his efforts to establish churches.

WHAT ABOUT THOSE LEFT BEHIND?

Of course, not all the inhabitants of Judah and Jerusalem were taken off to Babylon. As noted above, many of the poorest were left behind in the land. In the immediate aftermath of the destruction, the Babylonians appointed a Jewish man named Gedaliah as governor. But not long after being installed, Gedaliah was murdered by a rebel leader named Ishmael, who took a number of those left in the land (including Jeremiah) captive and headed for the land of the Ammonites. But Johanan, a leader of the rebel forces hiding out in the countryside, chased down Ishmael and rescued the captives (though Ishmael managed to escape).

At this point Johanan and the captives were faced with a choice: remain in the land or flee to Egypt. They asked Jeremiah to inquire of the Lord to find out what they should do, swearing,

> May the LORD be a true and faithful witness against us if we do not act according to all the word with which the LORD your God sends you to us. Whether it is good or bad, we will obey the voice of the LORD our God to whom we are sending you, that it may be well with us when we obey the voice of the LORD our God. (Jeremiah 42:5-6)

But when God commands them to remain in the land, Johanan and the rest of the leadership balk, denying that the Lord spoke to Jeremiah. They stubbornly head for Egypt, taking Jeremiah captive with them. At several points along this journey, the Lord warns the people through Jeremiah that instead of finding security in Egypt, they will face destruction. But the warnings go unheeded. The people double down on their rebellion and idolatry, and as a result Yahweh swears he will wipe them out in Egypt. At this point the story fades to black, and this group of exiles disappears from the biblical story.

CONCLUSION AND APPLICATION

With the land conquered, the temple destroyed, the Davidic dynasty dethroned, and most of God's people living in exile in a pagan land, it would be easy to lose hope altogether. But in addition to warning about the certainty of his coming judgment, the Lord also made staggering promises about restoring a remnant of his people on the other side of exile. In the next chapter we will look at some of those promises and consider to what extent they were fulfilled when a remnant did in fact return from exile.

But before moving on, we would be wise to reflect on how we as God's people today face challenges similar to those experienced by the exiles. Those of us living in the West face an increasingly secularized culture that grows more hostile to God, his people, and his ways. As this trend continues, God's instructions to his exiled people will continue to take on increasing relevance to us. While we may never face such direct challenges to compromise faithful obedience to the Lord as Daniel and his friends, we are daily faced with the temptation to compromise even in small matters of personal integrity. At the same time, the triumph of evil in the world around us can lead us to despair and question whether God will ever fulfill his promises to restore all things. Such despair can show itself in a deep-seated pessimism that constantly expects the worst to happen, or in a cynical smugness that prides itself in being "realistic" about the world around us. Either way, it is an expression of unbelief, for we serve a God who has promised not only to be with us but ultimately to right every wrong. And he calls us to be a light in the midst of that darkness, distinguished by our faith in him and our unshakable confidence in his power and faithfulness.

Chapter Four

RETURN FROM EXILE
WHEN ISRAEL REPENTS

AS WE SAW IN THE LAST CHAPTER, the exile was every bit as bad as God had promised. Maybe even worse. But through his prophets, Yahweh had also promised that exile would not be the final word. A day would come when God would restore his people from their exile and return them to the Promised Land. But what God promised was more than simply a physical return to the land where things returned to normal. He promised a new normal. A new normal that would return creation to an Edenic state and then beyond.

PREDICTIONS OF RESTORATION

From Israel's earliest days, God had made staggering promises of blessing for obedience alongside stern and foreboding warnings of judgment for disobedience. In fact, at numerous points God had indicated that disobedience and judgment culminating in exile would in fact come; it was only a matter of time. But alongside this dire warning came the promise of an eventual restoration in which Israel would be brought back to their land.

We see this reality as early as Leviticus 26:40-45. Israel is still at Sinai, though now in the aftermath of their idolatrous rebellion with the golden calf. In the midst of the various stipulations of the Mosaic covenant, God lays out a series of blessings for obedience (Leviticus 26:1-13) and curses for disobedience (26:14-39). But even when they will be sent into exile, it will not be the final word. God promises,

> Yet for all that, when they are in the land of their enemies, I will not spurn
> them, neither will I abhor them so as to destroy them utterly and break my
> covenant with them, for I am the LORD their God. But I will for their sake
> remember the covenant with their forefathers, whom I brought out of the
> land of Egypt in the sight of the nations, that I might be their God: I am the
> LORD. (Leviticus 26:44-45)

Within the promise of restoration, the key elements of the promise made to Abraham are present. God promises to bring his people out of the land of their enemies as they humble their uncircumcised hearts and confess their iniquities. He promises to remember the place that he promised to them and return them to the land after it has enjoyed its Sabbaths. But the culminating promise is his presence. He will be their God—the Lord who brought them out of Egypt in fulfillment of his promise to Abraham, Isaac, and Jacob. As the covenant-keeping God, Yahweh can be trusted to keep his promises.[1]

God makes a similar promise as Israel sits on the plains of Moab preparing to enter the Promised Land after forty years of wandering in the wilderness. Deuteronomy 27–28 reiterates the blessings for obedience and the curses for disobedience, which leads to a renewal of the covenant (Deuteronomy 29). Yet God makes it clear that it is only a matter of time before Israel experiences the curse of exile. So he prepares them for this future reality by saying,

> And when all these things come upon you, the blessing and the curse, which
> I have set before you, and you call them to mind among all the nations where
> the LORD your God has driven you, and return to the LORD your God, you

---

[1]See Allen P. Ross, *Holiness to the Lord: A Guide to the Exposition of the Book of Leviticus* (Grand Rapids, MI: Baker Academic, 2002), 481.

and your children, and obey his voice in all that I command you today, with all your heart and with all your soul, then the LORD your God will restore your fortunes and have mercy on you, and he will gather you again from all the peoples where the LORD your God has scattered you. (Deuteronomy 30:1-3)

Notice again our three key features of the Abrahamic promise, this time even further expanded from the similar passage in Leviticus 26:40-45. God promises to regather his people from the various nations where he has scattered them. He will circumcise their hearts so that they will wholeheartedly love Yahweh and obey all his commandments (Deuteronomy 30:6, 8). The Lord will make them even more numerous than their fathers (30:5). God will bring them back to the land (place) where he will cause their livestock and the land itself to be fruitful (30:9). Although God's presence is not specifically mentioned, it seems implied in the statement that God will delight in prospering them.[2]

Take another look at this passage. Do you see the language of Eden here? Just as God commanded Adam and Eve to be fruitful, multiply, and fill the earth, so now he promises to make the people fruitful. Just as God made the garden for Adam and Eve to dwell in with the Lord, so now God promises they will dwell in the land with him. Just as God connected blessing with obedience in the garden, so now in this restoration God's people will obey the Lord with all their heart and experience his blessing.

These promises of restoration on the front side of exile—given centuries before it actually happened—establish a foundation that the prophets who came after Moses would build on. As God's covenant lawyers, they regularly call the people back to the promises God had made with his people, warning them of judgment for breaking the covenant and offering salvation for those who repent and remain faithful to Yahweh. But just as Moses had warned in the days before his death, the people refused to listen (Deuteronomy 31:24-29).

---

[2]Compare the conclusion of Roy E. Ciampa, who argues that this passage "describes the restoration of Israel in terms of the fulfillment of both the blessings promised to Abraham and those of the Mosaic covenant (possibly echoing Eden as well)." "The History of Redemption," in *Central Themes in Biblical Theology: Mapping Unity in Diversity*, ed. Scott J. Hafemann and Paul R. House (Grand Rapids, MI: Baker Books, 2007), 275.

FOUR KEY RESTORATION PROMISES

In the centuries leading up to the exile, God repeatedly sent his servants the prophets to repeat and expand on his promises of restoration after exile. The scope and number of these promises is well beyond what we can fully discuss here. But in looking at these prophetic passages, we can see four broad areas where God promised not merely to restore the people to the kind of life they experienced before exile but to usher in a new era of existence that would be like a return to Eden, only much better.[3]

Temple. The psychological shock resulting from the destruction of Solomon's temple is hard to put into words (though Lamentations gives us a taste). God had promised that he would dwell among his people, with the temple as the focal point of his presence. But those hopes were dashed when the Babylonians destroyed that temple in 586 BC.

Yet within the restoration promises given before the exile was God's announcement of a renewed (or, perhaps more precisely, a transformed) temple. During the eighth century, both Isaiah 2:2-4 and Micah 4:1-5 foresaw this reality, using almost the exact same wording. Let's look at Isaiah's version:

> It shall come to pass in the latter days
> > that the mountain of the house of the LORD
> shall be established as the highest of the mountains,
> > and shall be lifted up above the hills;
> and all the nations shall flow to it,
> > and many peoples shall come, and say:
> "Come, let us go up to the mountain of the LORD,
> > to the house of the God of Jacob,
> that he may teach us his ways
> > and that we may walk in his paths."
> For out of Zion shall go forth the law,
> > and the word of the LORD from Jerusalem. (Isaiah 2:2-3)

---

[3]Along separate but similar lines, N. T. Wright identifies temple, land, torah, and racial identity as the key symbols of the first-century Jewish worldview. See N. T. Wright, *Christian Origins and the Question of God*, vol. 1, *The New Testament and the People of God* (Minneapolis: Fortress Press, 1992), 224-32.

The phrase "latter days" points to the realization of this promise during the age of eschatological fulfillment.[4] Referring to the temple as the house of the Lord reminds the hearer that what makes the temple special is that God dwells there, not the structure itself. In the era of eschatological fulfillment, the mountain on which the temple sits will be the focal point of not just Israel but of all the nations. They will stream to the house of the Lord to learn the ways of Yahweh.

But had the exile changed God's plans for a transformed temple? Absolutely not. About thirteen years after the Babylonians leveled the temple, God gave the prophet Ezekiel an extended vision of a new temple (Ezekiel 40–48). Interpreters have long debated how best to understand the language of these chapters. Regardless, we can point out several key points from these chapters. First, the use of Edenic imagery to describe this new temple suggests that it goes well beyond a mere physical structure toward a restoration of creation that goes beyond its original sinless state (41:18-20; 47:6-12). That seems indicated by the description of the river flowing from the new temple that transforms saltwater bodies into fresh water and provides fruit for food and leaves for healing (47:6-12; Revelation 22:1-5). Second, the central thrust of these chapters is that God will once again dwell in the midst of his people. The glory of Yahweh that departed in anticipation of exile now returns to fill this new temple (Ezekiel 43:1-9), and the book ends with the statement "And the name of the city from that time on shall be, The LORD Is There" (48:35). Finally, there are at least hints that some Gentiles will be included in this restoration. God gives instructions for sojourners to be treated as the native-born children when it comes to allotting the inheritance of the land (47:21-23).

Torah. The fundamental issue that led to both Israel and Judah being sent into exile was breaking the covenant through persistent and flagrant idolatry. They failed to obey God's law and thus suffered his judgment. Yet even in the midst of such persistent disobedience to God's covenant law, Yahweh announced a coming day when not only the Jewish people but even the nations

---

[4]On the eschatological significance of this phrase in Isaiah 2:2, see G. K. Beale, *A New Testament Biblical Theology: The Unfolding of the Old Testament in the New* (Grand Rapids, MI: Baker Books, 2011), 103-5.

would pursue and experience a greater level of obedience to God's will. As we saw above in Isaiah 2:2 (cf. Micah 4:1-5), the purpose of Israel and the nations streaming to the house of the Lord is to learn his ways. The purpose of learning those ways is to be able to walk in them. The very thing that sinful and rebellious humanity had not been doing would become a reality "in the latter days."

In the waning days of Judah, the prophet Zephaniah foresaw a similar reality. After announcing the future conversion of the nations, Yahweh says,

> On that day you shall not be put to shame
>> because of the deeds by which you have rebelled against me;
> for then I will remove from your midst
>> your proudly exultant ones,
> and you shall no longer be haughty
>> in my holy mountain.
> But I will leave in your midst
>> a people humble and lowly.
> They shall seek refuge in the name of the LORD,
>> those who are left in Israel;
> they shall do no injustice
>> and speak no lies,
> nor shall there be found in their mouth
>> a deceitful tongue.
> For they shall graze and lie down,
>> and none shall make them afraid. (Zephaniah 3:11-13)

Instead of flagrantly rebelling against God's commandments, this renewed people will be purified from their pride and be marked by humble submission to Yahweh, seeking refuge in his name. Instead of pursuing injustice and lies, they will be marked by justice and truth. As a result, they will dwell in peace and security rather than shame and fear.

Turf. If God's people are to be restored from exile, they must return to the land of promise. God promises just such a return in numerous places, but we will focus our attention on the eighth-century prophet Hosea. After a lengthy description of God's impending judgment for idolatry (Hosea 2:1-13),

Yahweh vows to betroth himself to his people in a new exodus and remove the names of foreign gods from their lips (2:14-17). Then he promises,

> And I will make for them a covenant on that day with the beasts of the field, the birds of the heavens, and the creeping things of the ground. And I will abolish the bow, the sword, and war from the land, and I will make you lie down in safety. And I will betroth you to me forever. I will betroth you to me in righteousness and in justice, in steadfast love and in mercy. I will betroth you to me in faithfulness. And you shall know the LORD. (Hosea 2:18-20)

What Yahweh promises here goes well beyond a simple return to the land; even the land itself will be transformed. Borrowing creation language from Genesis 1,[5] Yahweh promises to eliminate any threat of conflict and warfare from the land so his people can dwell there securely. The Lord will bless the land with abundant fruitfulness so that it will produce grain, wine, and oil (Hosea 2:21-23). Just as God brought his people into the land after the original exodus, so after this new exodus he will sow them into the land as an act of sheer mercy. The covenant relationship that had been broken because of Israel's idolatry will be restored through a new covenant that extends to creation itself.

This promise of a transformed land when God restores his people is even clearer in other texts. Isaiah 51:3 states that when Yahweh comforts Zion (by restoring her from exile), he will also make "her wilderness like Eden, her desert like the garden of the LORD; joy and gladness will be found in her, thanksgiving and the voice of song." When the Lord restores his people to the land, they will say, "This land that was desolate has become like the garden of Eden, and the waste and desolate and ruined cities are now fortified and inhabited" (Ezekiel 36:35). The transformation will be so dramatic that even the mountains themselves will drip with sweet wine, the hills will flow with milk, and the streams will be full of water (Joel 3:18; Amos 9:13-15).

Throne. When the people are restored from exile, they will live under the rule of a king from David's line. As we have seen, God had promised David a line of descendants that would culminate in a king who would reign over

---

[5]On the Edenic language and imagery used here, see Duane A. Garrett, *Hosea, Joel*, NAC 19A (Nashville: Broadman & Holman, 1997), 86-96.

an eternal kingdom (2 Samuel 7:12-16). But that hope seemed to potentially run aground when the nation split into two kingdoms, with only the Southern Kingdom of Judah ruled by a Davidic descendant. Even that sliver of hope seemed taken away when Judah was sent into exile. But well in advance, God had promised that part of restoring his people would involve giving his people a Davidic king:

> "In that day I will raise up
>   the booth of David that is fallen
> and repair its breaches,
>   and raise up its ruins
>   and rebuild it as in the days of old,
> that they may possess the remnant of Edom
>   and all the nations who are called by my name,"
>   declares the LORD who does this. (Amos 9:11-12)

The booth of David refers to the royal house of David, which will be restored along with God's people. A descendant of David will rule over this restored people of God, and his rule will encompass not merely the land of Israel but Edom and even the nations. Under his rule even creation itself will be transformed (Amos 9:13-15).

Numerous other texts share this hope of a king from David's line ruling over God's restored people in a restored land. Hosea 3:5 foresees a day when "the children of Israel shall return and seek the LORD their God, and David their king, and they shall come in fear to the LORD and to his goodness in the latter days." Isaiah 11:1-10 anticipates a Spirit-anointed descendant of David who will reign in righteousness and justice over Israel and the nations. In Jeremiah 23:5, Yahweh promises that "I will raise up for David a righteous Branch, and he shall reign as king and deal wisely, and shall execute justice and righteousness in the land." God's purposes for Israel and ultimately all of humanity will be realized through a Davidic king.

Conclusion. These four promises of temple, torah, turf, and throne do not capture every promise God makes related to restoration from exile, but they do capture the main emphases. These four restoration promises also embody the foundational components of people, place, and presence. The promise of people finds fulfillment in a renewed people who are marked by heightened obedience to Yahweh. At the same time, it also focuses hope on a singular descendant who will reign on David's throne. The promise of place shows up in the hope of not merely returning to the land in security but also in the transformation of the land into an Edenic state. Finally, the promise of presence comes through in the hope of a new temple where God dwells with his people.

THE NEW COVENANT

In addition to these various promises related to temple, torah, turf, and throne, God promises a new covenant, or what is sometimes called an everlasting covenant or a covenant of peace. This new covenant encompasses the three key features of people, property, and presence and will be the means by which God reverses the exile of not only Israel and Judah, but the nations as well. Let's look at this new covenant and its relationship to God's promise of restoration from exile in each of the three major prophets.[6]

Isaiah 40–55. Isaiah 40 opens with a call of comfort for God's people in anticipation of the good news that the end of exile has come and God will establish his kingdom.[7] Israel was called to be Yahweh's servant to be a light to the nations (Isaiah 42:1-8), but instead became blind and deaf because of their sin and was therefore sent into exile (42:18-25). As a result, God promises to do a new thing. Not only will he bring his people out of exile; he will even transform creation itself (43:18-28) and pour out his Spirit on his people (44:1-5). Yahweh can accomplish this redemption because he is the only true God, in contrast to the idols the nations worship (44:6-20).

Yahweh will bring this promised salvation by raising up a new individual servant who will obey where Israel failed (Isaiah 49:1-12). This servant will regather Israel out of their exile and also be a light of salvation to the nations.[8]

---

[6]For helpful discussions of the new covenant in these three major prophets, see Peter J. Gentry and Stephen J. Wellum, *Kingdom Through Covenant: A Biblical-Theological Understanding of the Covenants* (Wheaton, IL: Crossway, 2012), 433-530.

[7]Throughout Isaiah 40–55, the prophet frames the people's sin and resulting exile in Deuteronomic terms; for further detail, see Matthew S. Harmon, *She Must and Shall Go Free: Paul's Isaianic Gospel in Galatians*, BZNW 168 (Berlin: de Gruyter, 2010), 207-8.

[8]Ciampa ("History of Redemption," 272-73) notes that in Isaiah, Israel's return to the land is regularly linked to the nations coming to Israel to worship their God and serve their people (e.g., Isaiah 42:1, 6; 49:5-7, 22; 60:1-16).

Yahweh will fulfill his promise to Abraham and ultimately transform creation itself when he reveals his saving righteousness and brings his people back to the land (51:1-16). God's people are called to announce the good news that Yahweh is establishing his kingdom by redeeming Israel from exile and bearing his mighty arm in the sight of all the nations (52:7-12). But the means by which the Lord will accomplish this redemption and establish his kingdom is shocking. Rather than a conquering king, God will use a suffering servant, who takes on himself the curse God's people deserve for their sins and is vindicated with an inheritance (52:13–53:12).[9]

In response to the servant's work, God's redeemed people are called to sing and rejoice because they are so numerous that they must expand where they are living (Isaiah 54:1-3). Instead of fear and shame, they will delight in their husband, Yahweh, and his love for them (54:4-8). Just as God swore to Noah never again to destroy the earth with a flood, so now he swears that his anger toward them has been spent (54:9). The reason for Yahweh's anger ceasing is given in the following verse: "'For the mountains may depart and the hills be removed, but my steadfast love shall not depart from you, and my covenant of peace shall not be removed,' says the Lord, who has compassion on you." (54:10).

When the servant redeems his people from exile, Yahweh will establish a "covenant of peace" rooted in his steadfast love and compassion. Unlike the covenant that Israel broke (leading to their exile), this covenant will endure even if creation does not. As a result of this covenant of peace, God's people will dwell securely in the land as vindicated servants of Yahweh (54:11-17).

In light of this glorious work of redemption accomplished by the servant and the covenant of peace he establishes, Yahweh now invites everyone who thirsts and hungers to experience the blessings of his redemption (55:1-2).

---

[9]The suffering that the servant experiences is specifically described in terms borrowed from Deuteronomy 27–30, showing that the servant is suffering for Israel's sin that led to exile. See Anthony R. Ceresko, "The Rhetorical Strategy of the Fourth Servant Song (Isaiah 52:13–53:12): Poetry and the Exodus-New Exodus," *CBQ* 56 (1994): 42-55 (esp. 47-50); G. P. Hugenberger, "The Servant of the Lord in the 'Servant Songs' of Isaiah: A Second Moses Figure," in *The Lord's Anointed: Interpretation of Old Testament Messianic Texts*, ed. P. E. Satterthwaite, Richard S. Hess, and Gordon J. Wenham (Grand Rapids, MI: Baker Books, 1995), 129-39; Harmon, *She Must and Shall Go Free*, 144-45.

Those who respond to this invitation will receive the covenant promises made to David (55:3). This "everlasting covenant" is another way of referring to the covenant of peace in Isa 54:10. It is rooted in Yahweh's covenant love for David (i.e., 2 Samuel 7:12-16), signaling that this suffering servant is also a Davidic king. Because of this everlasting covenant, everyone (including the Gentile nations) is summoned to seek Yahweh and find forgiveness for their sins (Isaiah 55:4-7). This marvelous good news is so beyond human reasoning that it can only be an act of God to accomplish it (55:8-11). Even creation itself will rejoice at its transformation, and the name of Yahweh will become an everlasting sign that will never be cut off (55:12-13).[10]

Thus, in Isaiah the new covenant that results from God restoring his people from exile is an outworking of God fulfilling his covenants with Abraham and David. God accomplishes this great work of redemption that transforms creation itself through a servant who obeys where Israel fails and suffers the curse they deserve for their sin. God will pour out his Spirit on his people to dwell with them, and even the nations will participate in the kingdom that God will establish through this everlasting covenant of peace.

Jeremiah 31. The only place in the Old Testament where the exact expression "new covenant" occurs is in Jeremiah 31. After reaffirming the basic covenant promise ("I will be the God of all the clans of Israel, and they shall be my people"), Yahweh promises to restore his people (Jeremiah 31:1-6). As a result, they should rejoice at this news (31:7-9). The nations are warned about this future restoration (31:10-14), but exiled Judah is so discouraged that God must reassure them it will indeed come to pass (31:15-26). Yahweh will sow his redeemed people back into the land, watching over them to build and plant just as he had done to pluck up and break down (31:27-30). Then the Lord announces the new covenant:

> Behold, the days are coming, declares the LORD, when I will make a new
> covenant with the house of Israel and the house of Judah, not like the cov-
> enant that I made with their fathers on the day when I took them by the
> hand to bring them out of the land of Egypt, my covenant that they broke,

---

[10]Ciampa notes that in the prophets (including Isaiah) exile is portrayed as a return to chaos and de-creation, while restoration is portrayed in terms of a new creation in which the Spirit produces a return to Edenic blessings. "History of Redemption," 273-74.

though I was their husband, declares the LORD. For this is the covenant that I will make with the house of Israel after those days, declares the LORD: I will put my law within them, and I will write it on their hearts. And I will be their God, and they shall be my people. And no longer shall each one teach his neighbor and each his brother, saying, "Know the LORD," for they shall all know me, from the least of them to the greatest, declares the LORD. For I will forgive their iniquity, and I will remember their sin no more. (Jeremiah 31:31-34)

At the heart of this passage is the familiar covenant formula in which Yahweh promises to be their God and they will be his people. But the emphasis clearly falls on how this new covenant will be different from the Mosaic covenant that Israel broke through their idolatry. Three differences in particular stand out. First, rather than write the law on tablets of stone, in the new covenant God will write the law directly on the hearts of his people. Second, in this new covenant everyone in the covenant community will know Yahweh. Under the Mosaic covenant, a large number of people were part of the covenant community through birth and circumcision but did not know the Lord. Third, whereas the Mosaic covenant offered continual sacrifices to cover sin, in this new covenant Yahweh will provide complete and final forgiveness for his people.

In the chapters that follow, Jeremiah expands on the nature of this new covenant. God's renewed people will dwell securely in the land (Jeremiah 32:37). Even more significantly, Yahweh promises, "I will give them one heart and one way, that they may fear me forever, for their own good and the good of their children after them" (32:39). God will establish this new covenant through the work of a descendant of David, who will rule in righteousness and justice (33:14-18). In keeping this promise, Yahweh would be acting to fulfill not only his promise to David but also his promise to Abraham, Isaac, and Jacob (33:25-26).

Thus, in Jeremiah the new covenant has elements of both continuity and discontinuity with the Mosaic covenant. Most notably, this new covenant will be eternal in nature and involve the internalization of God's law within his people. Full and final forgiveness will come, and a descendant of David will rule over God's people in fulfillment of his promises.

Ezekiel 34–37. As the prophet living with the exiles in Babylon, the promises of restoration would have been especially sweet to Ezekiel. In chapters 34–37, God gives Ezekiel a series of visions that highlight different aspects of the new covenant he would establish with his people. In contrast to the wicked shepherds who exploit God's people in Ezekiel's day, a day is coming when God himself will shepherd his people through a descendant of David and establish a covenant of peace that will result in the land producing abundant fruit, echoing Edenic language (Ezekiel 34:1-31).

Ezekiel expands this vision of a new covenant in chapter 36. Yahweh will multiply people and beasts in the land and do more good to them than ever before, all for the sake of vindicating the holiness of his name (Ezekiel 36:1-21).[11] Then comes this summary of the new covenant:

> I will take you from the nations and gather you from all the countries and bring you into your own land. I will sprinkle clean water on you, and you shall be clean from all your uncleannesses, and from all your idols I will cleanse you. And I will give you a new heart, and a new spirit I will put within you. And I will remove the heart of stone from your flesh and give you a heart of flesh. And I will put my Spirit within you, and cause you to walk in my statutes and be careful to obey my rules. You shall dwell in the land that I gave to your fathers, and you shall be my people, and I will be your God. (Ezekiel 36:24-28)

As part of bringing his people back to the land, he will cleanse them from all their sins, including the idolatry that led to exile in the first place. Yahweh will perform heart surgery on his people, taking out the heart of stone— hardened through their rebellion—and replacing it with a heart of flesh that will be responsive to him. But even more significantly, God will put his very own Spirit in his people to cause them to obey! Yahweh will be their God, and they will be his people, living in a renewed land that will be like the Garden of Eden (Ezekiel 36:33-36).

Ezekiel 37 approaches restoration from exile in a slightly different way. Yahweh will resurrect his people to cause them to dwell in the land (37:1-14).

---

[11]Ciampa notes that the restoration of Israel described in Ezekiel 36:8-12 enables the fulfillment of both Adams' original commission (Genesis 1:26-31) and the promises to Abraham (Genesis 12:1-3). "History of Redemption," 274.

God will unite Judah and Israel into one renewed people who live in the land (37:15-23). Then comes this summary:

> My servant David shall be king over them, and they shall all have one shepherd. They shall walk in my rules and be careful to obey my statutes. They shall dwell in the land that I gave to my servant Jacob, where your fathers lived. They and their children and their children's children shall dwell there forever, and David my servant shall be their prince forever. I will make a covenant of peace with them. It shall be an everlasting covenant with them. And I will set them in their land and multiply them, and will set my sanctuary in their midst forevermore. My dwelling place shall be with them, and I will be their God, and they shall be my people. Then the nations will know that I am the LORD who sanctifies Israel, when my sanctuary is in their midst forevermore. (Ezekiel 37:24-28)

This everlasting covenant of peace combines elements we have already seen in the previous Ezekiel passages. Generations of God's people will live in the land securely under the rule of a Davidic king. They will be characterized by a heightened level of obedience to the Lord. Yahweh will put his sanctuary in their midst and dwell with them in this renewed land. The covenant formula is once again repeated. This restoration will be so dramatic and miraculous that even the nations will know "that I am the LORD who sanctifies Israel."

Thus, in Ezekiel this everlasting covenant will result in Yahweh both dwelling in his people by his Spirit and in the midst of his people. A Davidic ruler will shepherd God's people in a renewed land for generation after generation. This renewed people will embody a heightened level of obedience because God puts in them a new heart and causes them to walk in his ways. This is not merely a renewed nation of Israel; it is a renewed humanity that will be placed in a new Eden.[12]

Conclusion. The problem of sin (particularly idolatry) was so deeply rooted in God's people that exile was necessary. But God remained committed to fulfilling his promise to Abraham as the means by which he would ultimately

---

[12]Stephen G. Dempster, *Dominion and Dynasty: A Biblical Theology of the Hebrew Bible*, NSBT 15 (Downers Grove, IL: InterVarsity Press, 2003), 169-72; see also N. T. Wright, *Christian Origins and the Question of God*, vol. 3, *The Resurrection of the Son of God* (Minneapolis: Fortress Press, 2003), 119-21.

end humanity's exile and bring them back to a place where he could dwell
with them. The key elements of people, place, and presence that were forfeited
in the garden and promised in the covenant with Abraham would be fulfilled
in a new and everlasting covenant of peace.

NOT WHAT THEY EXPECTED

In 538 BC the Persian king Cyrus announced a decree allowing the Jews to
return to their homeland and build a temple for the Lord (Ezra 1:1-4). But it
doesn't take long to realize that this return is not everything they hoped it
would be in light of God's promises. Far from being a multitude of people
streaming back to the land, the total number of returning exiles is about fifty
thousand people (Ezra 2:64-65). Despite having the authorization of King
Cyrus, the returnees faced immediate opposition. Something just is not right.
In fact, a quick look at the four key promises of temple, Torah, turf, and
throne makes it clear that although they are back in the land, this was not
the restoration they were expecting.[13] Elements of the restoration promises
seem to be inaugurated in some sense, yet the full realization of those promises
are in some sense postponed.

Temple. Shortly after the first wave of exiles returns to Jerusalem, they
begin rebuilding the temple (Ezra 3:1-9). But when they finish laying the
foundation it becomes apparent that this new temple will not come close to
matching Ezekiel's vision. In fact, it isn't even as big as Solomon's temple. So
while some shouted with joy upon the foundation's completion, "many of the
priests and Levites and heads of fathers' houses, old men who had seen the
first house, wept with a loud voice when they saw the foundation of this house
being laid" (3:12). To make matters worse, the surrounding peoples begin to
mount significant opposition to the rebuilding of the temple, and they manage
to successfully halt construction for nearly seventeen years (4:1-5).

But God was not done with this temple rebuilding project. He raises up
the prophets Zechariah and Haggai to call the people back to the project
(Ezra 5:1-3; Zechariah 1:1-6; Haggai 1:1–2:23). After five years of hard work
in the face of continued opposition, the rebuilt temple is finally completed

---

[13]On this "return" falling far short of being *the return*, see John Goldingay, *Old Testament Theology*,
vol. 1, *Israel's Gospel* (Downers Grove, IL: InterVarsity Press, 2003), 725-26.

and dedicated (Ezra 6:13-18). Shortly afterward the people celebrate by keeping the Passover festival (6:19-22).

The temple is now rebuilt, but it clearly does not measure up to what the prophets had foretold. Besides the obvious discrepancy in the dimensions of the temple itself, two additional observations in particular make this clear. First, the celebration marking the rebuilt temple pales in comparison to the one celebrating Solomon's temple. Whereas Solomon's temple was dedicated with the sacrifice of 22,000 oxen and 120,000 sheep (1 Kings 8:63), all the returned exiles can muster is 100 bulls, 200 rams, 400 lambs, and 12 goats (Ezra 6:17). But second, and more significantly, God's glory never descends to fill this rebuilt temple with his presence. When Solomon brought the ark of the covenant into the temple, "a cloud filled the house of the LORD, so that the priests could not stand to minister because of the cloud, for the glory of the LORD filled the house of the LORD" (1 Kings 8:10-11). Nowhere in any of the biblical books written after the exile is there any mention of God's glorious presence filling the temple. Yes, Yahweh reassures his people he is with them as they rebuild the temple (Haggai 2:4-5) and even promises "in a little while" to fill this house with his glory (2:6-9). But had this happened, it is difficult to imagine such an event not being recorded in Ezra, Nehemiah, or any of the postexilic prophets such as Haggai, Zechariah, or Malachi. Although the temple is rebuilt, it pales in comparison to what was promised. More importantly, God's presence never fills it. Surely there must be more to come.

Torah. At the center of God's promised restoration through a new covenant was a renewed and obedient people who would have God's law written on their hearts and his Spirit dwelling in them causing them to obey. But even a quick surface-level reading of the biblical books written after the people return to the land makes it clear this promise is not a reality. In Malachi 3:5 (probably the latest Old Testament book written), God warns,

> Then I will draw near to you for judgment. I will be a swift witness against the sorcerers, against the adulterers, against those who swear falsely, against those who oppress the hired worker in his wages, the widow and the fatherless, against those who thrust aside the sojourner, and do not fear me, says the LORD of hosts.

Far from describing a renewed and obedient people, it is clear that many of the problems that plagued Israel and Judah before the exile are still alive and well among the returned exiles. This lack of obedience shows itself in four primary ways.

First, and probably most prominently, is interacting with foreigners among the surrounding peoples. The main way this problem manifested itself was through marriage (Ezra 9:1–10:44; Nehemiah 13:1-3, 23-29; Malachi 2:10-16). Both Ezra and Nehemiah rebuke the people for this breach of the covenant. God was not against intermarriage on ethnic grounds, but religious ones. In other words, these marriages were condemned because the foreigners they were marrying worshiped other gods. Nehemiah makes the point that if even the great king Solomon was led astray from Yahweh because of foreign wives who worshiped other gods, why should they think they will fare any better (Nehemiah 13:27)?

Second, the various regulations for temple service are not being followed. Because the Levites were not receiving the required offerings from the people, they were forced to abandon service in the temple to provide for their own needs (Nehemiah 13:10-14). Instead of offering spotless animals as sacrifices, the priests were offering blemished animals (Malachi 1:6–2:9). Instead of trusting Yahweh by bringing in the required tithes and offerings, some of the people were selfishly holding on to their resources (3:6-12). At one point they even provided a chamber in the temple for a foreigner (Nehemiah 13:4-9)!

Third, some of the people were failing to observe the Sabbath (Nehemiah 13:15-22). Some were treading wine, while others were transporting goods such as grain, wine, and figs into the city to sell them. Foreigners were also bringing in goods for sale on the Sabbath. Only when Nehemiah stations armed guards at the gates of Jerusalem does the practice come to an end.

Fourth, the poor were being oppressed (Nehemiah 5:1-13). In an effort to pay their taxes and provide for their growing families, some of the poorest people began to mortgage their fields and borrow money from wealthier Jews at interest. When that was insufficient, they began to sell their sons and daughters into slavery. Nehemiah must step in to end this financial oppression and begin the process of restitution.

These snapshots make it clear that the promise of a renewed and obedient people has not been realized. No wonder the final prophetic word of the Old Testament ends with this combination of warning and promise:

> Remember the law of my servant Moses, the statutes and rules that I commanded him at Horeb for all Israel. Behold, I will send you Elijah the prophet before the great and awesome day of the LORD comes. And he will turn the hearts of fathers to their children and the hearts of children to their fathers, lest I come and strike the land with a decree of utter destruction. (Malachi 4:4-6)

Turf. The people may be back in the land, but it is certainly not the land they expected. Based on what the prophets had foretold, the people expected to live in the land of promise with borders that rivaled or even surpassed what Israel experienced during the reign of Solomon. Yet when the first wave of exiles returned to the land, they were returning to the Persian province of "Beyond the River," which encompassed much of what had been Samaria and Judah. The city of Jerusalem was a shadow of what it had been. During the height of the Southern Kingdom, Jerusalem had become a large city as successive kings expanded it into a significant urban center in the region. But in the aftermath of three Babylonian campaigns, Jerusalem had been reduced to less than half of what it had been, returning to the modest size it was when David conquered the city.

Not only was the size of the land significantly smaller but they were far from living in peace and security. From the moment the exiles returned to the land, they faced constant opposition from the surrounding peoples. After starting the rebuilding of the temple, these surrounding peoples thwarted construction for over fifteen years (Ezra 4:1-5). Nehemiah arrived nearly a century later to rebuild the city walls, and he faced opposition from the surrounding people even though he had direct authorization from the Persian emperor himself (Nehemiah 4:1-23).

Throne. On top of the fact that the returned exiles were living in a territory far smaller than what God had promised, they remained under the thumb of a foreign power. Instead of a righteous and just Davidic king ruling over them, they were subject to the whims and wishes of a foreign king and regional governor. Nehemiah sums up the situation clearly at the end of his lengthy prayer of confession:

> Behold, we are slaves this day; in the land that you gave to our fathers to enjoy its fruit and its good gifts, behold, we are slaves. And its rich yield goes to the kings whom you have set over us because of our sins. They rule over our bodies and over our livestock as they please, and we are in great distress. (Nehemiah 9:36-37)

Slaves instead of free people. The bounty of the land sent off to foreign rulers. Their bodies and their livestock subject to the whims of pagan authorities. Great distress rather than everlasting joy. Surely this cannot be the fulfillment of God's promises.

CONCLUSION AND APPLICATION

As the Old Testament draws to a close, the people are back in the land. But it is evident to everyone that God's promises of restoration through a new covenant inaugurated by a Davidic descendant remain unfulfilled.[14] Yes, some elements of the restoration promises seem to be inaugurated, but their full realization remains postponed for the future. For the next four hundred years things more or less remain the same. The Jews remain a political football between regional powers—Persians, Greeks, Ptolemies, and Seleucids. True, they do regain their independence for nearly a century through the Maccabean revolt, and the scope of the territory they control does reach Solomonic levels. But the temple is far from being a focal point the nations are streaming toward to worship Yahweh. The people are not marked by a heightened level of obedience to the torah. And they are not ruled over by a Davidic descendant. Because of political unrest and intrigue,

---

[14]There is significant scholarly debate over the extent to which people during the period between the close of the Old Testament and the opening of the New Testament (a period of nearly four hundred years!) still saw themselves in a state of exile. For the argument that central to the Jewish worldview of the first century was the belief that Israel was still in exile, even though a remnant had returned to the land of Israel beginning in the late sixth century BC, see N. T. Wright, "Yet the Sun Will Rise Again: Reflections on the Exile and Restoration in Second Temple Judaism, Jesus, Paul, and the Church Today," in *Exile: A Conversation with N.T. Wright*, ed. James M. Scott (Downers Grove, IL: IVP Academic, 2017), 19-80. But a survey of Jewish literature suggests that most Jews believed that return from exile had at least been inaugurated to some extent; see Ciampa, "History of Redemption," 286-90.

the Romans are actually invited to come in and clean up the mess (63 BC),
something they are more than happy to do. They appoint rulers over the
Jewish people to keep the peace and ensure a steady flow of tax revenue to
the ever-expanding Roman Empire. Some accepted Roman rule, while
others resisted. Even when circumstances seem calm on the surface,
rebellion and unrest are always lurking below the surface. Hope and
expectation ebbed and flowed, but it was never extinguished.[15] Surely
Yahweh had not given up on his people, had he? Then a man named John
the Baptist appears in the Judean wilderness, preaching a baptism of
repentance for the forgiveness of sins and announcing that the promises of
restoration were on the verge of being fulfilled.

We often find ourselves in a similar position of waiting for God to fulfill
his promises. As we will see in the next chapter, the promises of restoration
began to be fulfilled through the life, ministry, death, resurrection, and ascension of Jesus. But we must wait for his return to consummate the promises
of temple, torah, turf, and throne. It is this reality that is "our blessed hope,
the appearing of the glory of our great God and Savior Jesus Christ" (Titus 2:13).
Even in the midst of sorrow, disappointment, brokenness, and suffering,
our lives should be marked by an unshakable hope that is both an anchor
for our lives (Hebrews 6:19) and fuel for patiently waiting for God to fulfill
his new creation promises (Romans 8:18-25).

---

[15]For an extended discussion of Jewish hopes in the period leading up to the New Testament, see
Wright, *New Testament and the People of God*, 280-338.

Chapter Five

THE END OF EXILE INAUGURATED THROUGH JESUS' LIFE AND MINISTRY

SOMETIMES THE MOST SIGNIFICANT EVENTS in our lives have remarkably small and seemingly insignificant beginnings. While some people can remember the very moment they met their spouse, others cannot. Only in looking back can they notice the beginnings of a relationship that would eventually change their lives.

In a sense that was the case with the arrival of Jesus. In retrospect, it is easy to look back and see the significance of what Jesus was doing to inaugurate the end of exile.[1] But in the moment it would have been easy to misunderstand what Jesus was doing since it did not exactly look like what the Jewish people were expecting.

---

[1]To be clear, I am not suggesting, as does N. T. Wright, that return from exile is the central motif or master paradigm for understanding everything that Jesus said and did.

THE MINISTRY OF JOHN THE BAPTIST

John the Baptist stepped into the explosive context of Roman rule over the land of Israel and Jewish hopes for restoration through a messiah. Around AD 29 he began wandering the Judean wilderness near the Jordan River. According to Luke 3:3, John was "proclaiming a baptism of repentance for the forgiveness of sins." Our familiarity with a statement like this can blind us to its significance. God had promised that if Israel, while in exile among the nations, would return to Yahweh by loving him with their whole heart and soul and obey his voice, he would take delight in restoring them (Deuteronomy 30:1-10). In other words, Israel's path to restoration involved repentance. As part of the new covenant that he would institute with his restored people, God had promised to forgive their iniquity and remember their sin no more (Jeremiah 31:34). Embedded within this description of John's message is the announcement that the promised restoration from exile was about to begin.

Luke shows that we are on the right track with this interpretation by explaining John's actions with a citation of Isaiah 40:3-5:

As it is written in the book of the words of Isaiah the prophet,

"The voice of one crying in the wilderness:
   'Prepare the way of the Lord,
   make his paths straight.
Every valley shall be filled,
   and every mountain and hill shall be made low,
and the crooked shall become straight,
   and the rough places shall become level ways,
and all flesh shall see the salvation of God.'" (Luke 3:4-6)

These verses come immediately after Yahweh announces comfort to his people that their iniquity has been pardoned and comfort for Jerusalem is coming (Isaiah 40:1-2).[2] They also set the stage for explaining how God will accomplish the restoration of his people: through a servant who obeys where

---

[2] By citing Isaiah 40:3-5, Luke is drawing on the larger context of Isaiah 40–55 and God's promise of restoring Israel and humanity from exile. See David W. Pao, *Acts and the Isaianic New Exodus*, Biblical Studies Library (Grand Rapids, MI: Baker Books, 2002), 41-45.

Israel failed and becomes a light of salvation to the nations through his suffering and vindication, which establishes an everlasting covenant in fulfillment of the promises to Abraham and David (Isaiah 40–55).

One final confirmation that John's message announced the coming restoration from exile is the summary statement that "with many other exhortations he preached good news to the people" (Luke 3:18). The Greek term translated "preach good news" (*euangelizomai*) is used at two key points in the Greek translation of the Hebrew Old Testament in Isaiah 40–55. The first is Isaiah 40:9, where God's redeemed people are described as a "herald of good news" announcing the arrival of God to redeem his people. The second is Isaiah 52:7, where the feet of those who announce the good news that Yahweh reigns are described as beautiful. The reign of Yahweh is the result of restoring his people from exile and bringing salvation to the nations through the suffering servant (52:13–53:12) instituting an everlasting covenant of peace that fulfills the promises to Abraham and David and results in the transformation of creation itself (54:1–55:13).

When John the Baptist began preaching a baptism of repentance for the forgiveness of sins, he was announcing that Israel's extended exile was finally coming to an end. And it would come to an end through the one coming after him—one who was greater and who would baptize with the Holy Spirit and fire (Luke 3:15-17).

THE LIFE AND MINISTRY OF JESUS

As part of bringing restoration from exile, God had promised that he would raise up a servant who would obey where Israel had failed (Isaiah 49:1-8). That is precisely how Matthew portrays Jesus in the opening chapters of his gospel account. Jesus is the one who relives Israel's experiences yet obeys where they had failed.[3]

We see this important theme right from beginning of the book. After introducing Jesus as the one who fulfills the promises made to both David and Abraham (Matthew 1:1), Matthew traces his genealogy. He structures the genealogy into three sections, with exile taking center stage (he explicitly

---

[3]For far more detail on this theme in Matthew, see G. K. Beale, *A New Testament Biblical Theology: The Unfolding of the Old Testament in the New* (Grand Rapids, MI: Baker Books, 2011), 406-23.

mentions it four times). The first is from Abraham through Jesse, the father of King David (1:2-6). The second is from David through "Josiah the father of Jechoniah and his brothers, at the time of the deportation to Babylon" (1:6-11). The final section runs from "after the deportation to Babylon" (1:12) through the birth of Jesus (1:16). Matthew then summarizes: "So all the generations from Abraham to David were fourteen generations, and from David to the deportation to Babylon fourteen generations, and from the deportation to Babylon to the Christ fourteen generations" (1:17).

Note that Matthew does not mention the return of some exiles to the land through the decree of the Persian king Cyrus. It is as if for Matthew it never even happened. But now that Jesus the Christ has arrived, return from exile can finally begin through the one who is both the son of Abraham and the son of David.[4] It is through this one named Jesus (whose name means "Yahweh saves") that God will save his people from their sins (1:18-25), which in light of the context of the genealogy and the citation from Isaiah 7:14 has in view (at least in part) Israel's sin that led them into exile.[5]

When wise men from the East appear before Herod to ask where to find the newborn king of the Jews, Herod asks the Jewish leaders where the Christ would be born. They respond by quoting Micah 5:2: "And you, O Bethlehem, in the land of Judah, are by no means least among the rulers of Judah; for from you shall come a ruler who will shepherd my people Israel" (Matthew 2:6, quoting Micah 5:2).

In its original context, God's promise of a shepherd to rule over his people is set against the backdrop of impending exile for Israel's covenant unfaithfulness. Through this shepherd from David's line, a remnant will dwell securely in the land.

---

[4]Matthew's decision to structure the genealogy with fourteen generations from Abraham to David, from David to exile, and exile to Jesus has been widely discussed. In addition to fourteen being a multiple of seven (which in the Bible is often presented as a number of perfection, completion, or fullness), Matthew may have based this decision on noting that the Hebrew letters of David's name add up to fourteen. See W. D. Davies and Dale C. Allison, *A Critical and Exegetical Commentary on the Gospel According to Saint Matthew*, ICC (New York: T&T Clark International, 2004), 1:163-65. If so, it is simply one more way of signaling that Jesus is the Son of David in whom the promises of God will find their fulfillment.

[5]Roy E. Ciampa, "The History of Redemption," in *Central Themes in Biblical Theology: Mapping Unity in Diversity*, ed. Scott J. Hafemann and Paul R. House (Grand Rapids, MI: Baker Books, 2007), 292.

When these Gentile wise men offer the Christ child their gifts, they do so in fulfillment of Psalm 72:8-11, a prayer expressing what kind of king the ultimate descendant of David will be:

> May he have dominion from sea to sea,
>   and from the River to the ends of the earth!
> May desert tribes bow down before him,
>   and his enemies lick the dust!
> May the kings of Tarshish and of the coastlands
>   render him tribute;
> may the kings of Sheba and Seba
>   bring gifts!
> May all kings fall down before him,
>   all nations serve him!

The arrival of this promised king will signal that God's purpose of humanity ruling over creation under his authority is coming to fruition (cf. Genesis 1:28). Through him the needy will be saved and the oppressed redeemed (Psalm 72:12-14). The land will produce abundant grain and fruit (Psalm 72:15-16; cf. Genesis 1:28; Deuteronomy 28:11-12). The name of this great king will endure forever and bring blessing to the nations, such that the entire earth will be filled with the glory of Yahweh (Psalm 72:17-19; cf. Genesis 12:1-3; 2 Samuel 7:12-16; Isaiah 11:9). For those steeped in the Old Testament hope, Matthew's account signals that this promised king has arrived.

Sometime after the wise men departed, an angel warns Joseph and Mary that Herod intends to kill the Christ child and that they must flee to Egypt (Matthew 2:13). In response they obey and remain in Egypt until Herod dies. Matthew explains that this happened to fulfill what the Lord spoke through Hosea: "Out of Egypt I called my son" (Matthew 2:15, citing Hosea 11:1). In its original context, Hosea 11:1 describes Israel's exodus out of Egypt. Matthew sees in that historical event a pattern that anticipates Jesus' own exodus out of Egypt—the promised new exodus that would end Israel's exile and bring restoration to God's people and creation itself. Matthew himself confirms this interpretation. In response to the grief caused by Herod's execution of children under two years old in Bethlehem, Matthew states that this happened to fulfill Jeremiah 31:15: "A voice was heard in Ramah, weeping and loud lamentation, Rachel weeping for her children; she refused to be comforted, because they are no more" (Matthew 2:18).

In its original context, this verse personifies the town of Bethlehem as Rachel, Jacob's second wife, who was buried nearby. She is weeping over the departure of the exiles on their way to Babylon. But in the verses that follow, God promises restoration to his people, culminating in a new covenant (Jeremiah 31:16-40). In a similar fashion, Bethlehem in Jesus' day weeps at the death of their children as a sign of their ongoing exile. But Matthew sees in the words of Jeremiah 31:15 and its larger context a pattern that anticipates not merely sorrow over death but restoration from exile.

Matthew's portrayal of Jesus as reliving Israel's experiences yet obeying continues with Jesus' baptism. On their way out of Egypt, Israel passed through the waters of the Red Sea (Exodus 14:1-31), and on their way into the Promised Land, Israel passed through the waters of the Jordan (Joshua 3:1-17). In a similar fashion, Jesus enters into the waters of the Jordan to be baptized; as a result the heavens open, the Spirit descends on him, and a voice from heaven identifies Jesus as the Beloved Son in whom the Father is well pleased (Matthew 3:13-17). God has called his son out of Egypt (2:15), and now he is announcing his identity as the servant of Yahweh and the anointed son of David (cf. Isaiah 42:1; Psalm 2:1-12) who will bring Israel's exile to an end. Matthew's description of the event also evokes language from Isaiah 63:11-15 and 64:1, which describe the first exodus in anticipation of a new exodus that would lead his people out of exile. The descriptions of waters parting, the presence of the Spirit, and placing people in a new land described in these two Isaianic texts themselves may echo the creation account of Genesis 1, which would link this new exodus to a new creation as well.

After Israel passed through the waters of the Red Sea, the Spirit of God led Israel, the son of God, into the wilderness. In a similar fashion, after passing through the waters of baptism in the Jordan, the Spirit leads Jesus, the Son of God, into the wilderness (Matthew 4:1-11). But unlike Adam, who failed in the garden, and Israel, who failed in the wilderness when tempted by Satan, Jesus obeys. Whereas Israel's hunger and thirst in the wilderness led them to grumble against the Lord and distrust him, Jesus' hunger and thirst led him to obey. In response to Satan's temptations, Jesus quotes three passages of Scripture from Deuteronomy 6–8. These chapters recount Israel's wilderness wanderings, highlighting their failures. By contrast, Jesus resists the temptations of Satan, showing that he is not only the obedient son of God but also the promised seed of Adam and Eve who would crush the serpent's head (Genesis 3:15). The new exodus that would lead to restoration from exile is under way!

Now that Jesus has passed his wilderness test, it is time for him to "enter the land" and begin his rightful rule over it (Matthew 4:12-17). Jesus settles in Galilee and establishes Capernaum as his ministry headquarters. Far from being a haphazard decision, this fulfills Isaiah 9:1-2:

"The land of Zebulun and the land of Naphtali,
> the way of the sea, beyond the Jordan, Galilee of the Gentiles—
the people dwelling in darkness
> have seen a great light,
and for those dwelling in the region and shadow of death,
> on them a light has dawned." (Matthew 4:15-16)

In its original context, Isaiah 9:1-2 looks forward to a day when God will bring his people out of the gloom and darkness of exile. God's people will rejoice in the fruitfulness of the land, and every vestige of their enemies will be gone (Isaiah 9:3-5). This restoration will come through a Davidic king who will rule over an eternal kingdom (9:6-7). By citing Isaiah 9:1-2, Matthew signals that Jesus is the promised Davidic king entering the land to restore them from their state of exilic darkness. Thus it should come as no surprise that Jesus begins proclaiming, "Repent, for the kingdom of heaven is at hand" (Matthew 4:17).

Now that Jesus has "entered the land," he begins to regather Israel around himself (Matthew 4:18-25). He starts by calling his first disciples, and in doing so he tells them, "Follow me, and I will make you fishers of men" (4:19). This statement is more than a simple analogy; it is an allusion to Jeremiah 16:16. The larger context promises that when Yahweh brings his people out of exile, they will no longer primarily identify him as the God of the exodus but as the God who brings his people back to the land he gave to their fathers (Jeremiah 16:14-15). In that day God will send out fishers and hunters to catch the people and hunters to gather them back to the land (Jeremiah 16:16).[6] When he eventually chooses twelve men to be his closest disciples (Mark 3:13-19), it becomes clear Jesus is reconstituting a restored people around himself, using these twelve men as the foundation of a restored Israel.[7] Jesus confirms this understanding when he says to his disciples, "Truly, I say to you, in the new world, when the Son of Man will sit on his glorious throne, you who have followed me will also sit on twelve thrones, judging the twelve tribes of Israel" (Matthew 19:28).[8] As the promised Davidic king, Jesus is sending out his fishers to gather his people from their exile and bring restoration through the arrival of God's kingdom. Or to use imagery from John, Jesus is the Good Shepherd who lays down his life to regather the lost sheep of Israel and the nations (John 10:1-18), just as Ezekiel 24:23-24 promised a Davidic shepherd king would do.

Now that Jesus the son of Abraham and son of David has arrived, Israel's restoration has begun. But this restoration will not simply address Israel's exile from the land; it will solve humanity's exile away from the presence of God that began back in the garden. To demonstrate that Jesus is in fact bringing about this promised restoration from exile, he provides several different kinds of signs for those who have eyes to see and ears to hear.

Jesus inaugurates restoration from exile through his ministry. Anyone can claim that the long-awaited restoration from exile was under way. Even his programmatic announcement that the kingdom of God was at hand and

---

[6]In a similar vein, Preben Vang sees in the sending out of the seventy (Luke 10:1-10) a background in the Table of Nations (Genesis 10), which would suggest that humanity's restoration from exile is under way; see C. Marvin Pate et al., *The Story of Israel: A Biblical Theology* (Downers Grove, IL: InterVarsity Press, 2004), 131-32.

[7]Craig Evans claims this is the strongest piece of evidence for the presence of exile theology in the Gospels. See Craig A. Evans, "Aspects of Exile and Restoration in the Proclamation of Jesus and the Gospels," in *Exile: Old Testament, Jewish, and Christian Conceptions*, ed. James M. Scott (Leiden, The Netherlands: Brill, 1997), 317-18. The story of the eleven apostles replacing Judas is further confirmation of the importance of these twelve men as the building blocks for restored Israel (Acts 1:12-26); see Pate et al., *Story of Israel*, 188-89.

[8]Helpfully noted by Preben Vang in Pate et al., *Story of Israel*, 130.

his call to respond by repentance has overtones of return from exile. But how could people possibly verify such claims? Throughout his ministry, Jesus performed three main kinds of signs to validate his message that the promised restoration from exile was under way.[9]

The first sign was healing. From the earliest days of his ministry, Jesus began healing "the sick, those afflicted with various diseases and pains . . . those having seizures, and paralytics" (Matthew 4:24). These healings were not simply to alleviate people's suffering; they were a preview of the new creation that God had promised would result from restoring his people from exile.[10] After noting that Jesus healed many sick people, Matthew claims he did so to fulfill what Isaiah 53:4 promised: "He took our illnesses and bore our diseases" (Matthew 8:17). As the suffering servant, Jesus brings healing as part of ending humanity's exile. Several chapters later, Matthew again connects Jesus' healing ministry with a servant of the Lord passage. Jesus' healing ministry fulfills Isaiah 42:1-3:

> "Behold, my servant whom I have chosen,
>> my beloved with whom my soul is well pleased.
> I will put my Spirit upon him,
>> and he will proclaim justice to the Gentiles.
> He will not quarrel or cry aloud,
>> nor will anyone hear his voice in the streets;
> a bruised reed he will not break,
>> and a smoldering wick he will not quench,
> until he brings justice to victory;
>> and in his name the Gentiles will hope." (Matthew 12:18-21)

---

[9]Craig Evans provides significant evidence from Second Temple Jewish texts that demonstrate the importance of signs to the Jews of Jesus' day. "Aspects of Exile and Restoration," 319-20. E. Randolph Richards suggests that John's Gospel places such emphasis on signs to signal that the messiah who would lead his people out of exile had finally come; see Pate et al., *Story of Israel,* 169-71.

[10]Compare the conclusion of James M. Scott, "Jesus' Vision for the Restoration of Israel as the Basis for a Biblical Theology of the New Testament," in *Biblical Theology: Retrospect and Prospect,* ed. Scott J. Hafemann (Downers Grove, IL: InterVarsity Press, 2002), 135: "Jesus' miracles and preaching were not simply acts of mercy; they were part of an agenda whose goal was the restoration of Israel. Jesus heralded that the works signaling the end of exile and the beginning of the restoration were being accomplished in and through his ministry to Israel."

Even more revealing is what Jesus says to the disciples of John the Baptist. It seems that Jesus was not quite doing exactly what John the Baptist had anticipated, so he sends these men to ask Jesus if he is the promised one or whether they should wait for another (Matthew 11:2-3). Jesus responds, "Go and tell John what you hear and see: the blind receive their sight and the lame walk, lepers are cleansed and the deaf hear, and the dead are raised up, and the poor have good news preached to them. And blessed is the one who is not offended by me" (Matthew 11:4-6).

Jesus' answer is more than a bullet point list of what he has been doing; it picks up language from several texts in Isaiah that promise physical healing in connection with God restoring his people from exile and transforming creation (Isaiah 29:18-19; 35:5-6; 61:1). Of these texts, Isaiah 35 seems especially pertinent. After promising the transformation of the desert at the revelation of God's glory in saving his people (35:1-4), the prophet writes,

Then the eyes of the blind shall be opened,
    and the ears of the deaf unstopped;
then shall the lame man leap like a deer,
    and the tongue of the mute sing for joy.
For waters break forth in the wilderness,
    and streams in the desert;
the burning sand shall become a pool,
    and the thirsty ground springs of water;
in the haunt of jackals, where they lie down,
    the grass shall become reeds and rushes. (Isaiah 35:5-7)

Physical healing is an expression of the same transformation that God will perform on creation itself. In that day, Yahweh will make a way in the wilderness for his people to pass through—"the Way of Holiness"—free from danger (Isaiah 35:8-9). As a result, God's ransomed people will return to Zion with singing and joy (35:10). By drawing on language from this passage, Jesus is telling the disciples to look around: the healings he is doing signal that the restoration of God's people from exile has begun and the promised new creation of God's kingdom is breaking into this fallen world.

A second sign that Jesus was inaugurating the promised restoration was exercising authority over the demonic realm.[11] The starting point for this is the wilderness temptation, where Jesus wins the opening battle in his war with the great serpent. As he continues to cast out demons, the Pharisees accuse him of casting out demons by the power of Beelzebul (another name for Satan). Jesus responds,

> Every kingdom divided against itself is laid waste, and no city or house divided against itself will stand. And if Satan casts out Satan, he is divided against himself. How then will his kingdom stand? And if I cast out demons by Beelzebul, by whom do your sons cast them out? Therefore they will be your judges. But if it is by the Spirit of God that I cast out demons, then the kingdom of God has come upon you. (Matthew 12:25-28)

Jesus begins by highlighting the absurdity of the charge before asserting that his casting out of demons by the Spirit of God shows that God's kingdom has arrived. He then portrays Satan as a strong man who has captured humanity and kept them in bondage. Jesus is likely alluding to Isaiah 49:22-26. God promises that the nations will bring his people back from their captivity so that his people will know that he is the Lord (49:22-23). He will bring judgment on their former captors and show that he is Yahweh, the Savior and Redeemer of his people (49:24-26). By casting out demons, Jesus is overcoming Satan the strong man and plundering his goods: the people whom he has kept in bondage because of their sin. Jesus is not only restoring Israel from its exile; he is restoring humanity from its exile. This conclusion seems confirmed by Jesus' reference to gathering and scattering, language that is regularly used in the Old Testament in connection with God restoring his people from exile (e.g., Deuteronomy 30:3; Jeremiah 31:10; Ezekiel 11:17; 20:34, 41; 28:25). Jesus is gathering his people to himself, bringing them out of their captivity to sin and Satan himself.

A final sign that Jesus has inaugurated the long-promised restoration was his teaching ministry.[12] God had promised in the latter days that people

---

[11]Rikki Watts argues that Jesus' defeat of the demonic authorities in Mark's Gospel is set against the backdrop of the Isaianic Yahweh Warrior motif. See Rikki E. Watts, *Isaiah's New Exodus in Mark*, Biblical Studies Library (Grand Rapids, MI: Baker Books, 2000), 140-69.

[12]One of the more debated aspects of N. T. Wright's use of return from exile as the central motif for understanding Jesus' work is his consistent interpretation of the parables through this lens;

would come to the Lord so that he could teach them his ways and walk in his paths (Isaiah 2:3) and that he would write his law on the hearts of his people (Jeremiah 31:33). So when Jesus begins traveling throughout the land of Israel teaching in their synagogues (Matthew 4:23) and in the temple courts (21:23), he is instructing his people how to live in this new creation kingdom he is establishing. When consulted privately by Nicodemus, Jesus insists that one must be born of water and the Spirit in order to enter God's kingdom (John 3:5), language that echoes God's promise to transform his people when he restores them from exile (Ezekiel 36:25-27).

Another way the gospel writers frame Jesus' teaching as part of bringing restoration from exile is by presenting him as a second Moses. We have already seen how Matthew 1–4 presents Jesus as reliving Israel's experiences yet obeying where Israel failed. After Jesus begins regathering his people through preaching the gospel, he goes up on a mountain to instruct the people on how they should live as God's people (Matthew 5:1–7:29).[13] In one sense Jesus is following in the footsteps of Moses, who also went up a mountain and taught Israel how they should live as God's covenant people (Exodus 20–31). But whereas Moses went up the mountain to receive God's instruction so he could pass it on to the people, Jesus himself gives the instruction as one who taught with his own authority. Jesus is like Moses—only better.

Moses himself had promised a day when God would raise up a prophet like him, only greater. As he was preparing the second generation of Israelites to enter the Promised Land, Moses said,

> The LORD your God will raise up for you a prophet like me from among you, from your brothers—it is to him you shall listen. . . . I will raise up for them a prophet like you from among their brothers. And I will put my words in his mouth, and he shall speak to them all that I command him. And whoever

---

for a helpful summary and perceptive critique, see Klyne R. Snodgrass, "Reading and Overreading the Parables in *Jesus and the Victory of God,*" in *Jesus & the Restoration of Israel: A Critical Assessment of N. T. Wright's Jesus and the Victory of God,* ed. Carey C. Newman (Downers Grove, IL: InterVarsity Press, 1999), 61-76. Thus, while Wright does offer some insightful readings of various parables, on the whole his effort to read every parable through this lens is unpersuasive.

[13]Ciampa contends that the Beatitudes are best understood as an expression of the fulfillment of Isaiah 61, which envisions how God's redeemed people were supposed to live when eschatological restoration arrived. "History of Redemption," 292-93. In doing so he follows Robert A. Guelich, "Matthean Beatitudes: 'Entrance-Requirements' or Eschatological Blessings?," *JBL* 95 (1976): 433.

will not listen to my words that he shall speak in my name, I myself will require it of him. (Deuteronomy 18:15, 18-19)

That Jesus is this prophet greater than Moses is evident not simply from the parallels in Matthew 1–7. The account of Jesus' transfiguration makes it crystal clear (Matthew 17:1-13). After Jesus' appearance was transformed before them, none other than Moses and Elijah appear. According to Luke 9:31, they were discussing with Jesus "his exodus, which he was about to fulfill in Jerusalem" (author's translation). Like Moses before him, Jesus is about to lead his people in a new exodus, out of their bondage to sin, death, and the devil. The Father's voice from heaven settles any doubt about Jesus' identity as the prophet greater than Moses: "He was still speaking when, behold, a bright cloud overshadowed them, and a voice from the cloud said, 'This is my beloved Son, with whom I am well pleased; listen to him'" (Matthew 17:5). Jesus is the beloved Son promised in Psalm 2; Jesus is the servant of Yahweh in whom the Father delights (Isaiah 42:1); and Jesus is the prophet greater than Moses who must be listened to as he leads his people in a new exodus out of their exile.

The feeding of the five thousand is further example of a miracle that presents Jesus as a Moses figure who is leading his people out of their exile in a new exodus, and John's account makes this especially clear (John 6:1-15). He notes that the Passover was near (6:4) and that Jesus asks Philip where they would find enough bread to feed the crowds as a test (6:6). Once the miracle is performed and everyone eats to their satisfaction, the crowd says, "This is indeed the Prophet who is to come into the world!" (6:14), a clear allusion to the promise of a prophet greater than Moses (Deuteronomy 18:15). They even begin to discuss forcing Jesus to be their king (John 6:15), suggesting that they see Jesus as not only a new Moses but possibly the promised descendant of David who would be the shepherd who feeds them as part of their restoration from exile (Ezekiel 34:23-24). Jesus is feasting with his people on the mountain as he leads them in a restoration that will one day swallow up death itself (Isaiah 25:6-9).[14]

---

[14]Noted helpfully in William L. Lane, *The Gospel According to Mark*, NICNT (Grand Rapids, MI: Eerdmans, 1974), 232.

CONCLUSION AND APPLICATION

Too often as believers we treat the life and ministry of Jesus as merely a prelude to the "real" work of Jesus accomplished by his death and resurrection. But what Jesus does during his life and ministry is more than live a sinless life so he can qualify to be our perfect substitutionary sacrifice on the cross. His signs are more than simply proof that he is who he claims to be. Through his life and ministry Jesus is obeying where both Adam and Israel before him had failed. Through his obedience and signs (healings, exorcisms, and teaching) Jesus inaugurates the return from exile that both Israel and humanity have been longing for. As N. T. Wright puts it:

> Healing, forgiveness, renewal, the twelve, the new family and its new defining characteristics, open commensality, the promise of blessing for the Gentiles, feasts replacing fasts, the destruction and rebuilding of the Temple: all declared, in the powerful language of symbol, that Israel's exile was over, and that Jesus was himself in some way responsible for this new state of affairs, and that all that the Temple had stood for was now available through Jesus and his movement.[15]

With the arrival of Jesus, the eschatological people of God are coming into existence!

Jesus obeying in our place is one of the sweetest truths of the gospel. All who trust in Jesus have his perfect obedience credited to them. We who could not meet the righteous demands of God's law have a Savior who came "to fulfill all righteousness" (Matthew 3:15). We who could not be perfect as our heavenly Father is perfect (5:48) have been given the perfect obedience of Jesus. Despite being tempted in every respect, he remained sinless (Hebrews 4:15), and is therefore able to help us when we are tempted (2:17-18).

The life and ministry of Jesus begin the end of exile for both Israel and humanity. But it takes more than obeying in our place to ransom humanity from its captivity to sin, death, and the devil and to restore us to the presence of God. Jesus must not only live for us, but he must die for us, rise for us, and ascend for us.

---

[15]Wright, *Jesus and the Victory of God*, 436, cited in Beach, *Church in Exile*, 114. In quoting this I am not claiming, as Wright does, that return from exile is the controlling and defining framework for understanding Jesus' ministry.

Chapter Six

RESTORATION THROUGH JESUS' DEATH, RESURRECTION, AND ASCENSION

SOMETIMES WE JUST DO NOT GET IT. No matter how many times we are told something, it just does not sink in. The doctor tells us that if we do not stop eating unhealthy foods, our cholesterol will continue to increase to dangerous levels. Yet we continue to consume greasy, fatty foods because we either think the doctor is wrong or we are simply unwilling to accept the truth that we must change how we eat in order to avoid potentially disastrous consequences.

Jesus found himself in a similar situation. As the time for his earthly ministry to end approached, Jesus repeatedly warned his disciples that when they arrived in Jerusalem, he would be handed over to the authorities, suffer, die, and rise from the dead (Matthew 16:21-23; 17:22-23; 20:17-19). But they simply did not get it. Their lack of understanding combined with their refusal to believe such a horrible thing prevented them from seeing the truth.

But far from being a tragic ending to the story of Jesus, his death, resurrection, and ascension are the culminating acts in his mission to restore his people from exile.

THE DEATH OF JESUS

Given the human and Satanic adversaries that Jesus faced, it was only a matter of time before they conspired to kill him. Yet deep within the mysterious counsel of God, this is exactly what the Lord had planned from the foundations of the earth (Acts 2:22-24; Ephesians 1:3-14). The death of Jesus would be the paradoxical means by which the offspring of the woman would crush the serpent's head (Genesis 3:15), obeying where Adam failed and paying the penalty humanity deserved for its rebellion against God. The sin that led to humanity's exile from God's presence would once and for all be decisively dealt with.[1] Through his death, Jesus would bring an end to the exile of both humanity in general and Israel in particular, leading them back into the very presence of God.

The New Testament presents and describes the death of Jesus from a variety of different angles to help us see the richness of what Christ did for us on the cross. Four in particular highlight Jesus' death as the means by which exile is brought to an end.

First, Jesus dies as the suffering servant promised in Isaiah. We have already noted a few places where Matthew cites one of the servant passages to explain some feature of Jesus' life and ministry (Isaiah 53:4 in Matthew 8:14-17; Isaiah 42:1-3 in Matthew 12:15-21). Now we will look at several texts where the death of Jesus is described in terms borrowed from Isaiah 52:13–53:12.

Mark 10:45 is a good place to begin. In the days leading up to Jesus' entry into Jerusalem for his death, two of his disciples (James and John) ask for positions of prominence in Jesus' kingdom (Mark 10:35-37). Even after Jesus mildly rebukes James and John, the remaining disciples

---

[1] N. T. Wright helpfully draws out the connection between forgiveness of sins and return from exile, but in doing so he is in danger of obscuring the forgiveness of sins that the individual experiences through the work of Jesus. See *Christian Origins and the Question of God*, vol. 2, *Jesus and the Victory of God* (Minneapolis: Fortress Press, 1996), 268-74.

are annoyed with them (Mark 10:38-41). Seizing this teachable moment, Jesus contrasts worldly authority and leadership with how they work in God's kingdom:

> You know that those who are considered rulers of the Gentiles lord it over them, and their great ones exercise authority over them. But it shall not be so among you. But whoever would be great among you must be your servant, and whoever would be first among you must be slave of all. For even the Son of Man came not to be served but to serve, and to give his life as a ransom for many. (Mark 10:42-45)

By referring to himself as a servant and a slave, Jesus identifies himself as the servant of Yahweh promised in Isaiah.[2] More significantly, Jesus describes the way he has come to serve as giving his life as a ransom for many. Isaiah 53:10-12 portrays the suffering servant as offering his life as a guilt offering for many, taking on himself their transgressions and sins, and ultimately dividing the spoils of his victorious vindication with the many. The servant does this to take on himself the curse of exile (not merely Israel's but humanity's as well) that resulted from rebellion against God. Through his sacrificial death he ransoms his people from their exile and restores them to a renewed land where they dwell with God under an everlasting covenant of peace (Isaiah 54:1-17). By describing his death in terms borrowed from Isaiah 53, Jesus signals that his death will in fact bring an end to Israel and humanity's exile.[3]

Luke 22:37 provides another indication that Jesus is the suffering servant who dies to bring an end to exile. In the moments after eating the Last Supper with his disciples, Jesus begins to prepare them for what is about to happen. After telling his disciples to acquire moneybags, knapsacks, and swords, Jesus explains why: "For I tell you that this Scripture must be fulfilled in me: 'And he was numbered with the transgressors.' For what is written about me has its fulfillment" (Luke 22:37). Jesus uses Isaiah 53:12 to explain what is about to happen to him in his death. He will be numbered

---

[2]For a thorough discussion of this claim, see Watts, *Isaiah's New Exodus in Mark*, 269-87.

[3]See similarly and at length Brant J. Pitre, *Jesus, the Tribulation, and the End of the Exile: Restoration Eschatology and the Origin of the Atonement*, WUNT 204 (Tübingen, Germany: Mohr Siebeck, 2005), 397-418.

with transgressors because he will take on himself the transgression of his people, and as a result he will bear the curse of exile away from the presence of God in their place.

The Gospels are not the only place where Jesus' death is described in terms borrowed from Isaiah 53; we see it at several points in the epistles as well. Perhaps the clearest example that is connected to sin, exile, and restoration is in Galatians 3:10-14.[4] In his efforts to dissuade Gentile believers from keeping the Mosaic law as part of pursuing justification before God, Paul warns that all who rely on works of the law are under a curse (Galatians 3:10). He grounds this assertion in a combined citation of Deuteronomy 27:26 and 28:58. Together these two verses describe the culminating curse of exile that will come on Israel when they break the covenant. In response to humanity's exile,

> Christ redeemed us from the curse of the law by becoming a curse for us—for it is written, "Cursed is everyone who is hanged on a tree"—so that in Christ Jesus the blessing of Abraham might come to the Gentiles, so that we might receive the promised Spirit through faith. (Galatians 3:13-14)

Paul borrows the language of Christ redeeming us from the curse of the law from Isaiah 53, where the servant takes on himself the curse of exile that Israel (and by extension humanity) deserves for rebellion against God. Through his sacrificial death the blessing of Abraham and the promised Spirit come to all who believe—Jew and Gentile alike.

There are a number of other texts that describe the death of Jesus in the language of Isaiah 53. But the ones discussed above are more than sufficient to show that Jesus dies as the suffering servant to end humanity's exile away from the presence of God by taking on himself the curse his people deserved.

Second, Jesus ends humanity's exile by drinking the cup of God's wrath (Matthew 26:36-46). Facing the overwhelming prospect of the cross, Jesus retreats to a familiar place with his disciples. While praying, Jesus asks, "My

---

[4]N. T. Wright argues that return from exile plays a major role in Paul's engagement with Scripture; see N. T. Wright, *Paul and the Faithfulness of God*, Christian Origins and the Question of God (Minneapolis: Fortress Press, 2013), 4:1441-79.

Father, if it be possible, let this cup pass from me; nevertheless, not as I will, but as you will" (Matthew 26:39).

In the Old Testament, the cup is used as a symbol of God's judgment that must be drunk.[5] More specifically, it is used several times as a symbol of God's wrath poured out by sending his people into exile. Isaiah 51:17 refers to those whom God will redeem out of exile as "you who have drunk from the hand of the LORD the cup of his wrath, who have drunk to the dregs the bowl, the cup of staggering." Jeremiah 25:15 refers to Jerusalem and Judah drinking the cup of God's wrath when God brought the Babylonians to destroy and send them into exile. Ezekiel 23:31-34 refers to Judah drinking the same cup of wrath that Israel drank before her. So when Jesus refers to a cup that he wishes would pass, he has in view the cup of God's wrath that his people deserved for their rebellion against him. As the one who is reliving Israel's experiences, he too must drink the cup of God's wrath, experiencing exile as a form of judgment just as Adam and Israel before him. Despite this horrifying prospect, Jesus chooses the path of obedience. He is the one who obeys where Adam and Israel had failed, even though it means his own death.

Third, Jesus brings humanity's exile to an end by dying at Passover. Passover was the festival that commemorated God bringing Israel out of their captivity in Egypt through Moses. In the account of the transfiguration, Luke has already noted that Moses and Elijah were discussing the exodus he was about to fulfill in Jerusalem (Luke 9:31). It was no coincidence that Jesus orchestrated the entirety of his ministry to culminate in arriving at Jerusalem to celebrate the Passover festival. Luke reinforces the Passover setting of the hours leading up to Jesus' arrest by specifically referring to the Passover six times in Luke 22:15, recounting the events leading up to the Last Supper. He wants to make sure the reader understands what Jesus is doing against the backdrop of Passover.

When the time finally comes for Jesus to eat the Passover meal, he begins by saying, "I have earnestly desired to eat this Passover with you before I suffer. For I tell you I will not eat it until it is fulfilled in the kingdom of God"

---

[5]Commenting on the parallel passage in Mark 14:32-42, Pitre argues that the cup in view here is linked to the cup at the Passover meal, and thus it is the cup of eschatological trials that would bring about Israel's ransom from exile through a new exodus. *Jesus, the Tribulation*, 478-91.

(Luke 22:15-16). The reason for Jesus' eagerness in eating this Passover meal is that it commemorates more than simply the original exodus; it memorializes the new exodus that he is about to accomplish for his people on the cross. Jesus makes this point even clearer later in the meal when he takes a cup of wine and says, "This cup that is poured out for you is the new covenant in my blood" (Luke 22:20). In Jeremiah 31:31-34 the new covenant was the culmination of God restoring his people from exile. In saying that the cup represents the new covenant in his blood, Jesus was indicating that his death was the means by which God would restore his people from their exile and captivity to sin.

John makes it clear in his description of Jesus' death that he is dying as the Passover lamb sacrificed for God's people. After noting that the Roman soldiers broke the legs of the two men crucified with Jesus to hasten their deaths, John says they saw that Jesus was already dead and therefore did not need to break his legs (John 19:31-33). Just to be sure, one of the soldiers pierced Jesus' side with his spear, confirming he was dead (John 19:34-35). John explains that "these things took place that the Scripture might be fulfilled: 'Not one of his bones will be broken.' And again another Scripture says, 'They will look on him whom they have pierced'" (19:36-37).

The first passage is Exodus 12:46, which describes the requirements for the Passover lamb. Citing this passage confirms that Jesus is indeed "the Lamb of God, who takes away the sin of the world" (John 1:29). The second Old Testament passage is Zechariah 12:10, which anticipates that when the time of eschatological fulfillment comes, people will look on Yahweh, whom they have pierced, and subsequently mourn (Zechariah 12:10-14). But in connection with this mourning, God will open a fountain in Jerusalem to cleanse his people from their sin (13:1). Jesus is thus both the Passover lamb slain for his people and the one who is pierced so that forgiveness is accomplished.

There is at least one final indication that the New Testament sees Jesus' death as a form of exile that he experiences on behalf of his people. In his last moments on the cross, Jesus cries out, "My God, my God, why have you forsaken me?" (Matthew 27:46). Jesus uses the words of David in Psalm 22:1 to express the distance from the Father he is experiencing as a result of him taking on himself the sin of his people. In other words, on the cross Jesus enters into exile away from the presence of God, just like Adam and Israel before him.

THE RESURRECTION OF JESUS

But it's not enough for Jesus to experience exile on behalf of his people; he must also experience restoration. That, at least in part, is what happens in the resurrection of Jesus. We have already seen that in Ezekiel 37:1-14 God gives the prophet a vision of a valley of dead bones that he must prophesy over. When he does so, the Spirit of God comes on these bones and brings them back to life with flesh and skin. God explains that these bones are the whole house of Israel, which he will raise from their graves and bring them back into the land. Yahweh is so committed to the promises he has made to his people that he is willing to raise them from the dead to fulfill them.

As the one who is reliving Israel's experiences yet obeying where they have failed, Jesus is raised from the dead to experience the restoration that God has promised to his people. Although the New Testament nowhere comes out and directly states this, that seems to be the point of the enigmatic story in Matthew 27:52-53: "The tombs also were opened. And many bodies of the saints who had fallen asleep were raised, and coming out of the tombs after his resurrection they went into the holy city and appeared to many."

Even though Matthew places this story immediately after recounting Jesus' death, it seems most likely that these events happened on the day of Jesus' resurrection.[6] Matthew borrows the language of Ezekiel 37:12-13 (as well as perhaps Isaiah 26:19 and Daniel 12:1-2) in describing these dead saints being raised to life to signal that the promised restoration has begun through the resurrection of Jesus. Israel's restoration has begun because the one who embodies everything Israel was supposed to be has been restored from the exile of death.

But the resurrection of Jesus does more than signal the restoration of Israel; it signals the restoration of humanity. Paul makes this clear in his lengthy discussion of the resurrection in 1 Corinthians 15:20-23:

---

[6]See the helpful discussion of this passage in D. A. Carson, "Matthew," in *The Expositor's Bible Commentary*, ed. Frank E. Gaebelein (Grand Rapids, MI: Zondervan, 1994), 581-83.

But in fact Christ has been raised from the dead, the firstfruits of those who have fallen asleep. For as by a man came death, by a man has come also the resurrection of the dead. For as in Adam all die, so also in Christ shall all be made alive. But each in his own order: Christ the firstfruits, then at his coming those who belong to Christ.

Adam's sin brought death into this world and resulted in being exiled from God's presence in the garden. As the one who obeyed where Adam had failed, Jesus was raised to new life after taking on himself the sin of his people (Jew and Gentile alike). He has crushed the serpent's head and dealt with the sin that sent humanity into exile away from the presence of God. As a result, all who are in Christ (i.e., united to him by faith) share in this resurrection.

We have also seen that several Old Testament texts connect restoration from exile with both resurrection and the transformation of creation itself. So it is not surprising that in the New Testament we see similar connections. In 2 Corinthians 5:14-15, Paul explains that "the love of Christ controls us, because we have concluded this: that one has died for all, therefore all have died; and he died for all, that those who live might no longer live for them- selves but for him who for their sake died and was raised."

Christ died and was raised for the sake of his people as the last Adam, the promised descendant of David, and the suffering servant who leads his people in a new exodus out of their captivity to sin and exile away from the presence of God. Based on this reality, Paul draws a conclusion:

Therefore, if anyone is in Christ, he is a new creation. The old has passed away; behold, the new has come. All this is from God, who through Christ reconciled us to himself and gave us the ministry of reconciliation; that is, in Christ God was reconciling the world to himself, not counting their tres- passes against them, and entrusting to us the message of reconciliation. (2 Corinthians 5:17-19)

The phrase "new creation" appears nowhere in the Old Testament. But the explanatory expression that follows ("the old has passed away; behold, the new has come") clearly comes from Isaiah 43:18-19, where it refers to God transforming creation as part of the new exodus his chosen people will experience in connection with their restoration from exile (Isaiah 43:16-21).[7] As a result, these people that God forms for himself are redeemed "that they might declare my praise" (43:21). In others words, those who are in Christ experience at a personal level the inauguration of the new creation because they share in Christ's resurrection. They are in turn entrusted with the message that God is bringing humanity out of its exile away from his presence and reconciling them to himself by dealing once and for all with their sin through Jesus Christ (2 Corinthians 5:20-21).

Paul provides further confirmation that we are on the right track in the verses that follow. God appeals through Paul and his ministry teammates, exhorting them not to receive God's grace in vain (2 Corinthians 6:1, which may be echoing Isaiah 49:3). To support this claim, Paul cites Isaiah 49:8, "In a favorable time I listened to you, and in a day of salvation I have helped you," and then concludes, "Behold, now is the favorable time; behold, now is the day of salvation" (2 Corinthians 6:2). In Isaiah 49:8 the favorable time and the day of salvation refer to the restoration that God will accomplish through his obedient servant. According to Paul, that day has dawned as a result of the resurrection of Jesus.

We find a similar connection in the other New Testament occurrence of the phrase "new creation." At the close of Galatians, Paul writes, "But far be it from me to boast except in the cross of our Lord Jesus Christ, by which the world has been crucified to me, and I to the world. For neither circumcision counts for anything, nor uncircumcision, but a new creation" (Galatians 6:14-15).

Through the death of Jesus this fallen world—suffering under the effects of the curse that came from Adam's sin—has been crucified. Jesus' death and resurrection has rescued believers from this present evil age (Galatians 1:4). All who trust in Christ are crucified with him; as a result, they no longer live, but Christ lives in them. Their ongoing life in this world is lived by faith in the Son of God, who loved them and gave himself for them (Galatians 2:20, using language echoing the death of the suffering servant in Isaiah 53). Thus "new

---

[7]On the Isaianic new exodus backdrop to this passage and its connection to Paul's use of reconciliation language here, see G. K. Beale, "The Old Testament Background of Reconciliation in 2 Corinthians 5–7 and Its Bearing on the Literary Problem of 2 Corinthians 6:14–7:1," in *Right Doctrine from the Wrong Texts? Essays on the Use of the Old Testament in the New*, ed. G. K. Beale (Grand Rapids, MI: Baker Books, 1994), 217-47.

creation" in Galatians 6:15 refers to the inaugurated experience of restoration from exile away from the presence of God, encompassing spiritual resurrection and Christ dwelling in his people through the Holy Spirit. In the very next verse, Paul then pronounces a blessing: "And as for all who walk by this rule, peace and mercy be upon them, and upon the Israel of God" (Galatians 6:16).

The apostle borrows language from Isaiah 54:10, which refers to God's covenant of peace that is the result of showing his people mercy. That covenant of peace is the result of the suffering servant taking on himself the sins of his people and being vindicated (Isaiah 52:13–53:12). New creation is the result of God dealing with the sin of his people and restoring them out of their exile away from his presence.

Once Jesus is raised from the dead to inaugurate the promised restoration, he must begin gathering those scattered in exile away from the presence of God. So he brings his disciples together and says this:

> All authority in heaven and on earth has been given to me. Go therefore and make disciples of all nations, baptizing them in the name of the Father and of the Son and of the Holy Spirit, teaching them to observe all that I have commanded you. And behold, I am with you always, to the end of the age. (Matthew 28:18-20)

As the risen son of David (Matthew 1:1) and the Son of Man (26:64; cf. Daniel 7:13-14), Jesus is now exercising the dominion over creation that Adam was supposed to exercise as God's image bearer but failed to do (Genesis 1:28). As the son of Abraham (Matthew 1:1), the risen Jesus is multiplying his people among all the nations (Genesis 1:28; 12:1-3), identifying them as his own through baptism in the name of the Father, the Son, and the Holy Spirit. As the prophet greater than Moses (Deuteronomy 18:15-19), the risen Jesus is creating an obedient people who have God's laws written on their hearts and walk in the power of his Spirit (Jeremiah 31:33; Ezekiel 36:26-27). And now that their sin has been dealt with, Jesus is present with his people "always, even to the end of the age." As Oren R. Martin summarizes, "In fulfillment of God's covenant promises, then, the disciples will enjoy the Lord's presence in their mission to possess all the nations of the earth, for Jesus will be with them always. . . . In other words, Jesus is Lord over both the land and his people."[8] For those with eyes to see and ears to hear, the end of exile and the promised restoration have indeed begun!

Now that we understand the connection between resurrection and Israel's restoration, the question the disciples ask Jesus in Acts 1:6 makes good sense. As they are spending time with the risen Jesus they ask, "Lord, will you at this time restore the kingdom to Israel?" Jesus' response is quite striking. He doesn't rebuke them for asking a stupid question. Instead he says,

> It is not for you to know times or seasons that the Father has fixed by his own authority. But you will receive power when the Holy Spirit has come upon you, and you will be my witnesses in Jerusalem and in all Judea and Samaria, and to the end of the earth. (Acts 1:7-8)

The first part of Jesus' answer is a gentle way of reminding the disciples that the Father will work out his purposes in his own timing. But the second part of his answer indicates how God is going to work out the restoration that Jesus has inaugurated through his resurrection. The Spirit (who was promised as a sign that restoration had come, Ezekiel 36:27; 37:14) will be poured out on them to empower them to take the message of restoration throughout the land of Israel and ultimately to the ends of the earth.[9] This last phrase alludes to Isaiah 49:6, where the servant of Yahweh is described as "a light for the nations, that my salvation may reach to the end of the earth." The risen Jesus—the promised servant of Yahweh—dwells in his people by his Holy Spirit to announce that all who trust in Jesus can be freed from their captivity to sin and exile away from God's presence.

THE ASCENSION OF JESUS

The ascension is an often overlooked aspect of what Jesus has done for his people.[10] Yet viewed from one perspective it is the final element of Jesus' own "restoration." Philippians 2:6-11 implies this when it describes Christ as the one

---

[8]Oren R. Martin, *Bound for the Promised Land: The Land Promise in God's Redemptive Plan*, NSBT 34 (Downers Grove, IL: InterVarsity Press, 2015), 128.

[9]Luke may allude to the promise of the Spirit in connection with Israel's restoration (Isaiah 32:15; 44:3-5) as well as the role of those restored from exile as witnesses (43:12). See Alan J. Thompson, *The Acts of the Risen Lord Jesus: Luke's Account of God's Unfolding Plan*, NSBT 27 (Downers Grove, IL: InterVarsity Press, 2011), 106-8.

[10]For a notable exception, see Peter C. Orr, *Exalted above the Heavens: The Risen and Ascended Christ* (NSBT 47; Downers Grove, IL: InterVarsity Press, 2019).

who, though he was in the form of God, did not count equality with God a thing to be grasped, but emptied himself, by taking the form of a servant, being born in the likeness of men. And being found in human form, he humbled himself by becoming obedient to the point of death, even death on a cross. Therefore God has highly exalted him and bestowed on him the name that is above every name, so that at the name of Jesus every knee should bow, in heaven and on earth and under the earth, and every tongue confess that Jesus Christ is Lord, to the glory of God the Father.

Paul begins by describing Christ as being equal with God. Yet he willingly chose to go into "exile" away from heaven by taking on human flesh. While living here on earth in exile from heaven, he lived a life of perfect obedience. As the servant of Yahweh, he took on himself the sins of his people and experienced the ultimate form of exile: death. Yet the Father raised him from the dead and highly exalted him with the name above every name. Thus, through his ascension into heaven Jesus is "restored" into heaven and into the very presence of the Father, yet with an even higher status than he had before the incarnation.

CONFIRMATION FROM ACTS

One way of confirming that we are on the right track is to look at the apostolic preaching in Acts. If Jesus understood his life, ministry, death, and resurrection in terms of restoring both Israel and humanity from their sin-induced exile, then we should expect that to be reflected in the various examples of preaching recorded in Acts.[11]

A good place to begin is Peter's sermon at Pentecost (Acts 2:1-41), which by the first century was not only a celebration of the wheat harvest but also commemorated the giving of the law at Sinai.[12] The gift of the Spirit enabling

---

[11]Because of space restraints, we will look at just three sermons. In addition to these three examples, restoration from exile motifs are present in James's speech at the Jerusalem Council (Acts 15:13-21, with a citation of Amos 9:11-12) and Paul's speeches before Jews in the temple courts (Acts 22:1-21), the Jewish Council (23:1-11), Felix (24:10-21), and Agrippa and Bernice (26:1-29). Alan Thompson argues that the accounts of the gospel going to the Samaritans (8:1-25) and the outcasts (8:26-40) are framed as steps in God's plan to restore Israel. See *Acts of the Risen Lord Jesus*, 112-18.

[12]David Pao goes so far as to argue that Acts 2 should be read through the lens of God regathering the exiles; see Pao, *Acts and the Isaianic New Exodus*, 129-31. Yet he also notes that the regathering of the exiles is not "the central theme of the New Exodus program in Acts" (131n78). For an

the disciples to speak in various languages so that the gathered crowds could understand the gospel message reverses God's judgment of confusing the languages and scattering the people at the Tower of Babel (Genesis 11:1-9). Furthermore, the list of nations represented (Acts 2:8-11) may echo the language of Isaiah 11:11, which describes God regathering his scattered people from exile. As Pao notes, "With the return of the Jewish people in the eschatological era, the hope of the restoration of Israel is beginning to find its fulfillment."[13]

Peter's sermon itself further reveals restoration from exile motifs. He chooses as his key text Joel 2:28-32, which foresees a day when God's presence would not merely dwell in a temple or rest on key figures but ultimately all of God's people, great and small.[14] The devout Jews present for Pentecost would naturally have connected Peter's claim that Jesus rose from the dead (Acts 2:22-32) with the promise of Ezekiel 37:1-14 linking resurrection with restoration from exile. The call to repent and be baptized in order to experience forgiveness for sins and receive the Holy Spirit may further allude to restoration promises that connect repentance with God's cleansing of his people and the gift of the Spirit (Deuteronomy 30:1-10; Ezekiel 36:24-28). That the promise is for those who are "far off" (Acts 2:39) echoes the promise of restoration in Isaiah 57:19, and Peter's exhortation to "save yourselves from this crooked generation" (Acts 2:40) may draw language from Deuteronomy 32:5, describing the wilderness generation in similar terms. These various Old Testament allusions and echoes make it clear that at least part of what Peter is communicating in his sermon is that the promised restoration from exile has begun through Jesus, and the proper response is repentance and faith.

Peter's sermon in Solomon's portico also contains several restoration-from-exile motifs (Acts 3:12-26). Jesus is the servant of the Lord who through his death and resurrection fulfills the promise made to Abraham

---

extensive treatment of Acts 2:1-41 with particular emphasis on the Old Testament citations and allusions, see Beale, *New Testament Biblical Theology*, 593-613.

[13]See Pao, *Acts and the Isaianic New Exodus*, 131; and Thompson, *Acts of the Risen Lord Jesus*, 109-12.

[14]Peter appears to have borrowed the phrase "in the last days" from Isaiah 2:2 and inserted it at the beginning of his citation from Joel 2:28-32. The final lines of Joel 2:32 show significant overlap with Isaiah 37:32, which clearly envisions a remnant returning from exile.

(Acts 3:12-15, 24-26; cf. Genesis 12:1-3; Isaiah 52:13–53:12). As in his previous sermon, Peter again calls the crowd to repent so that "your sins may be blotted out" (Acts 3:19). Peter likely borrows this language from Isaiah 43:18-21, where God promises to blot out the sins of his people when he restores them from exile and transforms creation. The "times of refreshing" that will come from the presence of the Lord (Acts 3:20) may echo Isaiah 32:15, which envisioned the Spirit being poured out in connection with restoration from exile and the dawn of the new creation.[15] The "restoring all things" (Acts 3:21) that will take place when Christ returns is another way of referring to the new creation that will consummate God's restoration of not only Israel but all humanity from their exile away from God's presence (cf. Matthew 17:11).[16] As the prophet greater than Moses (Acts 3:22-23; Deuteronomy 18:15-18), Jesus is leading his people in a new exodus out of their slavery to sin into the inaugurated new creation promised by the prophets.

Our final example of preaching in Acts is Paul's message in the synagogue at Pisidian Antioch (Acts 13:16-52). Similar to Peter's sermons, Paul highlights Jesus' resurrection, the forgiveness of sins, and the call to repentance as well as the fulfillment of the promises made to both Abraham and David. With regard to the latter, Paul not only alludes to 2 Samuel 7:12-16 (Acts 13:23) and quotes Psalm 2:7 (Acts 13:33) and Psalm 16:10 (Acts 13:35) but also cites Isaiah 55:3 (Acts 13:34). In its original context, Isaiah 55:3 is a call for all peoples to experience the redemption from exile accomplished by Yahweh's servant through his death and resurrection in fulfillment of the promises made to David. Several verses later, in an effort to explain the shift in ministry efforts to the Gentiles, Paul cites Isaiah 49:6: "I have made you a light for the Gentiles, that you may bring salvation to the ends of the earth" (Acts 13:47).[17]

---

[15]Pao, *Acts and the Isaianic New Exodus*, 132-35.

[16]Although the noun used here (*apokatastaseōs*) occurs nowhere else in the New Testament or Septuagint, the cognate verb *apokathistēmi* does occur in both the New Testament (Matthew 17:11; Mark 9:12) and, more significantly, in several Septuagint passages that deal with Israel's restoration from exile (Jeremiah 16:15; 23:8; 24:6; Ezekiel 16:55; Hosea 11:11).

[17]This citation corresponds to other allusions and echoes in Luke 2:32; 24:46-47; and Acts 1:8 to signal that the promised new exodus through the work of the Isaianic servant has begun. See further Pao, *Acts and the Isaianic New Exodus*, 84-100.

These are God's words to the servant of Yahweh, whom God raises up to restore both Israel and the nations from their exile away from God's presence. Thus, Paul sees his ministry as a fulfillment of this restoration promise.[18]

These snapshots of apostolic preaching provide more than enough to demonstrate that the work of Jesus was understood as the means by which God was bringing an end to Israel and humanity's exile.

CONCLUSION AND APPLICATION

Through his death and resurrection, Jesus has inaugurated the new creation as the place where he dwells with his people. But in the meantime, his presence lives inside his people wherever they go through the gift of the Spirit.

For those of us who are followers of Jesus, this is our identity. Apart from Jesus we are descendants of Adam, born into this world as rebels and languishing in exile away from God's presence. But the good news of the gospel is that by turning from our sin and trusting in Jesus, his obedience becomes our obedience. His death becomes our death. His resurrection becomes our resurrection. His ascension becomes our ascension. His Spirit comes to dwell in our lives. His return from exile becomes our return from exile.

But if Jesus has accomplished our restoration from exile, how should his followers live as they await the final consummation of all God's promises? That is what we will explore in the next chapter.

---

[18]On this, see Matthew S. Harmon, *She Must and Shall Go Free: Paul's Isaianic Gospel in Galatians*, BZNW 168 (Berlin: de Gruyter, 2010), 78-86, 106-22.

Chapter Seven

LIFE AS EXILES
IN A FALLEN WORLD

THE NEW TESTAMENT gives a number of different metaphors for the Christian life. Believers are soldiers who fight against spiritual forces of wickedness (Ephesians 6:10-20; 2 Timothy 2:3-4). They are athletes who train and compete (1 Corinthians 9:24-27; Hebrews 12:1-2). They are hard-working farmers who labor in this world to produce a spiritual harvest (John 4:35-38; 2 Timothy 2:6).

An often overlooked metaphor of the Christian life is that of exiles living in a place that is not our home. But how are believers still exiles if Jesus has brought an end to exile through his life, ministry, death, and resurrection? The answer is that while Jesus has already inaugurated the end of our exile, he has not yet consummated it. Although it seems paradoxical, the New Testament clearly teaches that in some sense we are simultaneously dwelling in the promised land of the new creation and yet living in exile. As we saw in the previous chapter, Jesus obeyed where Adam, Israel, and all of us had failed. He experienced God's wrath for us by going into exile. He was fully restored from that exile through his resurrection and ascended into heaven to sit at the right hand of the Father. As believers, we share in his life, death, resurrection, and ascension because we are united to Christ by faith.

Yet we still live in this fallen world that groans under the effects of the curse that came from Adam's disobedience. The glorious promise of a new heavens and new earth has not yet been fulfilled. We do not yet have the imperishable resurrection bodies that God has promised. Even though the penalty for our sins has been fully paid, we must continually wage war against sinful desires. Even though Satan has been defeated through Jesus' obedience and sacrificial death, we still must battle against the spiritual forces of wickedness at work in this world.

In other words, we as believers live in the tension between the already and the not-yet.[1] By faith we are united to Christ and experience in part the blessings he has promised. God has given us the Holy Spirit as "the guarantee of our inheritance until we acquire possession of it" (Ephesians 1:14). In the meantime, however, we live as exiles in this fallen world, citizens of God's kingdom who live in a place that is not our true home.

What does it look like for God's people to live as exiles? Let's take a look at several key New Testament texts that spell it out for us.

1 PETER

Without question 1 Peter gives the most attention to our experience as exiles. In the very opening sentence, Peter refers to his audience as "elect exiles of the Dispersion" (1 Peter 1:1). While some have argued that this expression specifically refers to Jewish believers, the remainder of the letter strongly suggests the recipients are predominantly Gentile believers (see 4:3-4).[2] Just as Israel lived in a land that was not their home for various periods of time, so too God's new covenant people, the church (made of Jew and Gentile alike),

---

[1]For more on the already/not-yet dynamic of the Christian life and how it shapes the life and ministry of the church, see Benjamin L. Gladd and Matthew S. Harmon, *Making All Things New: Inaugurated Eschatology for the Life of the Church* (Grand Rapids, MI: Baker Books, 2016).

[2]For a helpful and concise discussion of the issue, see Thomas R. Schreiner, *1, 2 Peter, Jude*, NAC 37 (Nashville: Broadman & Holman, 2003), 38-41. E. Randolph Richards argues that 1 Peter is a Diaspora letter that takes it cues from Jeremiah's letter to the Babylonian exiles (Jeremiah 29:1-32); see C. Marvin Pate et al., *The Story of Israel: A Biblical Theology* (Downers Grove, IL: InterVarsity Press, 2004), 240-45. Calling 1 Peter a Midrash on Jeremiah 29, however, goes beyond the evidence.

are now scattered throughout this world, living as exiles. The word Peter uses for exiles stresses the temporary nature of a person's stay in a foreign place, referred to here as "the Dispersion." This was a technical term for the scattering of the Jewish people, and Peter applies it to all believers living in this fallen world that is not their true home. Far from being happenstance, God has chosen believers for this status.

As the letter unfolds, Peter continues to use language that has overtones of exile and restoration. Believers have been born again to a living hope through the resurrection of Jesus and received an inheritance (1 Peter 1:3-5), realities that, as we have seen, have connotations of restoration from exile (cf. Ezekiel 37:1-14). The Old Testament prophets were serving present-day believers when they predicted "the sufferings of Christ and the subsequent glories," an expression that may echo the description of the suffering and vindicated servant of Isaiah 53 (1 Peter 1:10-12). As those who call God their Father, believers are called to

> conduct yourselves with fear throughout the time of your exile, knowing that you were ransomed from the futile ways inherited from your forefathers, not with perishable things such as silver or gold, but with the precious blood of Christ, like that of a lamb without blemish or spot. (1 Peter 1:17-19)

Paradoxically, believers are living in exile away from their true home (the new heavens and earth) even though they have been ransomed from their slavery to futility by the blood of Christ, who is their pure and spotless Passover lamb. Believers have been born again "through the living and abiding word of God" (1 Peter 1:22-23). This claim is grounded in a citation of Isaiah 40:6-8, which in its original context reassures its hearers of the certainty that God will in fact end Israel's exile and restore them (1 Peter 1:23-25). Peter confirms this connection when he asserts that "this word is the good news that was preached to you" (1:25). The good news that the apostles preach is what the prophet Isaiah had foretold—restoration from exile through a suffering and vindicated servant.

Echoes of exile and restoration continue in the next chapter. Peter describes believers as both living stones and a holy priesthood (1 Peter 2:4-5). He bases these statements on a citation of Isaiah 28:16, where God announces that

when he restores the remnant of his people he will establish a new foundation
for them, a chosen and precious cornerstone (1 Peter 2:6). But in contrast to
those who stumble over Jesus, the cornerstone of the new temple that God
is building, Peter asserts,

> But you are a chosen race, a royal priesthood, a holy nation, a people for his
> own possession, that you may proclaim the excellencies of him who called
> you out of darkness into his marvelous light. Once you were not a people,
> but now you are God's people; once you had not received mercy, but now
> you have received mercy. (1 Peter 2:9-10)

In these two verses, Peter assembles a collage of Old Testament phrases to
explain the identity of believers. The first four expressions (chosen race, royal
priesthood, holy nation, a people for his own possession) come primarily
from Exodus 19:5-6, where God describes what Israel will be if they keep the
terms of the Mosaic covenant. Yet the last half of 1 Peter 2:9 is essentially a
citation of Isaiah 43:20-21: "The wild beasts will honor me, the jackals and
the ostriches, for I give water in the wilderness, rivers in the desert, to give
drink to my chosen people, the people whom I formed for myself that they
might declare my praise."

This passage comes in the midst of an announcement that Yahweh will lead
his people in a new exodus out of their exile in Babylon (Isaiah 43:14-17). This
new act of God will transform creation itself (43:18-19). As a result of being
restored from exile, God's redeemed people will proclaim the excellencies of
the God who called them out of darkness into light. That, Peter says, is the
identity of the church: restored exiles who make known to the world the good
news that those who are enslaved to sin can be ransomed through Jesus Christ.[3]

All these various descriptions with overtones of exile and restoration in
1 Peter 1:1–2:10 set the stage for the central command of the letter in 2:11-12:

> Beloved, I urge you as sojourners and exiles to abstain from the passions of
> the flesh, which wage war against your soul. Keep your conduct among the
> Gentiles honorable, so that when they speak against you as evildoers, they
> may see your good deeds and glorify God on the day of visitation.

---

[3]The use of language from Hosea 1:9-10 and 2:23 in 1 Peter 2:10 further identifies believers as those
who have been restored from their exile away from the presence of God.

Every instruction Peter gives for living the Christian life in the remainder of the letter flows from this fundamental call to live out their identity as "sojourners and exiles." These two terms have overlapping meaning, both describing people who live in a place other than their home. They also occur together in Genesis 23:4, where Abraham describes himself as a "sojourner and foreigner" when speaking to the sons of Heth about a burial place for his wife, Sarah. Even though the land had been promised to Abraham, at the time he had no home in it. David also calls himself a "sojourner" and "guest" like his fathers before him (Psalm 39:12). Drawing on this Old Testament backdrop, Peter describes believers as those whose true home is in the new creation. Believers indeed reside in the new creation but in an already/not-yet manner. Even though we temporarily dwell in this fallen world, our true home is in the new creation.

Because believers are strangers and exiles in this fallen world, Peter gives two commands: (1) abstain from the passions of the flesh and (2) keep your conduct among unbelievers honorable.[4] Again, the already/not-yet reality of the Christian life emerges. The sinful passions that stem from our common ancestor Adam still remain active in the life of the believer and, if not intentionally counteracted, will show themselves in tangible actions. Indulging these sinful actions would not only offend the holy God who redeemed us but bring dishonor to the name of Christ among unbelievers. So even though believers have been freed from slavery to sin through the death of Jesus, sin remains an active power that must be aggressively fought.

Christians are to trace their lives according to the pattern that Christ left for them. This pattern is described in 2:22-25, where Peter borrows several phrases from Isaiah 53:

> He committed no sin, neither was deceit found in his mouth [Isaiah 53:9]. When he was reviled, he did not revile in return; when he suffered, he did not threaten [53:7], but continued entrusting himself to him who judges justly. He himself bore our sins in his body on the tree [53:4, 11], that we might die to sin and live to righteousness. By his wounds you have been

---

[4]Peter uses the term "Gentiles" here, but in the context it clearly refers to unbelievers rather than ethnicity.

healed [53:5]. For you were straying like sheep [53:6], but have now returned
to the Shepherd and Overseer of your souls. (1 Peter 2:22-25)

As the suffering servant, Jesus suffered unjustly at the hands of sinful
human beings. He did so to restore his people from the exile that their sins
had brought about. Through the preaching of the good news, believers have
returned to the Great Shepherd, another term that evokes imagery of restoration from exile under a Davidic Shepherd who feeds, guides, and rules over
them (cf. Ezekiel 34:11-16, 22-30).

The remainder of the letter further explains what it looks like to follow
these commands practically. In 1 Peter 2:18-25, the apostle instructs household
servants that when they suffer for doing good at the hands of an unjust master,
it is evidence of God's grace at work in their lives (2:18-20). Peter broadens
the scope of suffering for doing good beyond household servants to all believers in 1 Peter 3:8-25. Picking up language from 2:23, believers are blessed
when they bless those who revile them (3:9). Peter grounds this claim with
a citation of Psalm 34:12-16, which David wrote while he was living in exile
away from the land of Israel, feigning madness before Abimelech, king of
Gath (Psalm 34:1; 1 Samuel 21:10-15). To motivate believers to do good even
if it means suffering, Peter again reminds them of Christ's example
(1 Peter 3:18-25). Christians have been brought to God through Jesus' death,
resurrection, and ascension, realities that, as we have seen, are linked to our
restoration from exile.

But as we await the consummation of these realities during our time in a
world that is not our home, we must arm ourselves with the mindset of Christ
(1 Peter 4:1-6). Instead of living a life controlled by sinful passions, believers
are to orient their lives on the basis of God's will (4:1-2). Because we are a
new creation in Christ, we must no longer spend our time and energy in the
sinful patterns of behavior that characterized our life before Christ (4:3).
When we refuse to join in with unbelievers in these sinful activities, we should
expect to be ridiculed and even mocked for our refusal (4:4-5). Such suffering
should not come as a surprise to us, since we identify ourselves as followers
of a suffering Messiah (4:12); instead, we should rejoice because we will
experience God's eschatological Spirit in fresh ways and display God's glory

to those around us as we endure (4:13-18). As we suffer according to God's will, we can entrust ourselves to our faithful Creator while pursuing good and turning away from sin (4:19).[5]

A final hint of the exile theme surfaces at the closing of the letter. Peter writes, "She who is at Babylon, who is likewise chosen, sends you greetings" (1 Peter 5:13). By referring to Rome (where he is writing from) as Babylon, Peter is embracing the reality of living in exile in this fallen world. Just as Babylon was the capital of the world power who ruled over the Jews in their exile, so in Peter's day Rome exercised authority over this fallen world. Peter's point is that regardless of which empire rules, believers should live as exiles as they await their true home in the new heavens and earth.

From first to last, Peter portrays believers as sojourners and exiles in this fallen world. Through the work of Jesus Christ the suffering servant, believers have been formed into a renewed and redeemed people. As individuals and as a community, they are the place where God's Spirit dwells and manifests his presence. As they wait for God to consummate his promises, they must wage war against their sinful passions and live in a way that reflects their identity as God's people living in a foreign land. This perspective shapes the way Christians view those with authority over them, their family relationships, suffering for doing what is right, and even leadership within the church.

HEBREWS

The author of Hebrews writes to a group of Christians who, under increasing pressure from those around them, are in danger of falling away from the faith. As part of his strategy to encourage these believers to remain faithful to Christ, the author portrays believers as sojourners who, although they live in this fallen world, are on their way to their final rest in the heavenly Jerusalem. Using Psalm 95:7-11 as his starting point, the author reminds them what happened to the Israelites who rebelled against Yahweh in the wilderness (Hebrews 3:7–4:12). Because they disobeyed, they failed to enter the rest of the Promised Land. Based on their failure, the author warns, "Let us therefore

---

[5]Peter's call for the elders to shepherd God's people under the authority of Jesus the Chief Shepherd (1 Pet 5:1-5) may also echo God's restoration promise to shepherd his people (Ezekiel 34:11-31) in contrast to the evil shepherds of Ezekiel's day (34:1-10).

strive to enter that rest, so that no one may fall by the same sort of disobedience" (4:11). The warning works based on typology. Like the Israelites before them, believers are living in the wilderness of this fallen world on their way to a final rest in a new creation. Temptations to sin and rebellion remain a dangerous reality that believers must join together to fight against, empowered by God's Spirit.

As the author retells the story of Abraham in the famous "Hall of Faith" of Hebrews 11, the theme of living as sojourners resurfaces. Abraham went out to receive an inheritance, living "in the land of promise, as in a foreign land, living in tents with Isaac and Jacob, heirs with him of the same promise" (11:9). The reason Abraham was able to live as a sojourner is that "he was looking forward to the city that has foundations, whose designer and builder is God" (11:10). After a brief summary of Sarah's faith, the author of Hebrews pauses to summarize the common experience of God's people:

> These all died in faith, not having received the things promised, but having seen them and greeted them from afar, and having acknowledged that they were strangers and exiles on the earth. For people who speak thus make it clear that they are seeking a homeland. If they had been thinking of that land from which they had gone out, they would have had opportunity to return. But as it is, they desire a better country, that is, a heavenly one. Therefore God is not ashamed to be called their God, for he has prepared for them a city. (Hebrews 11:13-16)

The fact that Abraham looked beyond the Promised Land indicates that the land promise had a greater and/or universal fulfillment beyond the land of Canaan.[6] Core to the identity of God's people is their status as strangers and exiles. Even as they live in this world, they look forward to being in their true homeland. That homeland is not found on this earth; the country they yearn for is a heavenly one, the eternal new creation. God has prepared a city for his people that transcends any earthly kingdom. This perspective on life as God's people is not limited to these heroes of faith; it is presented as a paradigm for us today as followers of Jesus. Like these great men and women

---

[6]Oren R. Martin, *Bound for the Promised Land: The Land Promise in God's Redemptive Plan*, NSBT 34 (Downers Grove, IL: InterVarsity Press, 2015), 144.

before us, we too are strangers and exiles, on our way to a heavenly homeland that God has prepared for us.

But our status as strangers and exiles does not mean that our inheritance is only a future reality. Hebrews 12 draws a contrast between the Israelites at the foot of Mount Sinai and believers under the new covenant. Whereas Israel cowered in fear at the foot of Mount Sinai (Hebrews 12:18-21), we as believers have in one sense already entered the heavenly Jerusalem and the assembly of God's eschatological people through Jesus our mediator (Hebrews 12:22-24). Just as God had promised through the prophets (e.g., Isaiah 40–55), he has gathered his restored people in a renewed Jerusalem. Psalm 110—which Hebrews already has cited repeatedly—anticipated a day when the Messiah would rule from Zion as a king from David's line and a priest from Melchizedek's line. Now that Jesus has died and risen from the dead, that reign from Zion has begun. As members of the new covenant that Jesus Christ inaugurated through his death and resurrection, we join with the angels and the saints who have died before us to form the assembly of the firstborn who appear before a holy God in joyful worship. Thus, through our participation in the life of the church and in fellowship with other believers, we join with all of God's people (including those currently in heaven) in our worship of him through our mediator, Jesus Christ. The end of the exile that humanity experienced because of Adam and Eve's rebellion in the garden has now been inaugurated, with believers brought back into God's presence in anticipation of the full realization of these promises in the new heavens and new earth.

While we are most certainly exiles and strangers awaiting the consummation, even in the present we experience the initial blessings of our homeland. In other words, we live in the tension between the already and the not-yet.

JAMES

In a fashion similar to 1 Peter, James addresses his letter to "the twelve tribes in the Dispersion" (James 1:1). But unlike 1 Peter, most scholars believe James is writing to a Jewish Christian audience.[7] As part of restoring his

---

[7] For a helpful summary of the reasons, see Douglas J. Moo, *The Letter of James*, PNTC (Grand Rapids, MI: Eerdmans, 2000), 23-25. James M. Scott links James to the genre of a "covenantal diaspora letter" sent to the scattered people of God, in which "an authoritative center

people from exile, God had promised to regather the twelve tribes (e.g., Isaiah 11:11-12; Jeremiah 31:8-12; Ezekiel 37:21-22). This hope intensified in Jewish literature in the centuries leading up to Christ, as seen, for example, in the *Testament of Benjamin* 9:2: "Nevertheless, the temple of God will be in your portion, and the last (temple) will be more glorious than the first. And the twelve tribes will be gathered together there, and all the nations, until the Most High will send forth His salvation in the visitation of an only begotten prophet."[8]

By drawing on this Old Testament and Jewish hope and referring to these Jewish believers as the twelve tribes, James identifies them as part of the restoration that Jesus has accomplished through his life, ministry, death, resurrection, and ascension.

Yet James also indicates that these twelve tribes are "in the Dispersion." He uses this term in the same way Peter did—as a technical term for the scattering of the Jewish people as a result of exile. Unlike Peter, however, James seems to be using it to refer specifically to Jewish believers who are scattered outside the land of Israel.

Thus, by describing these Jewish believers as "the twelve tribes in the Dispersion," James brings together the already/not-yet dynamic of their restoration. On the one hand, they are indeed part of the eschatological people of God, reconstituted as a redeemed people through the work of Jesus, the true Israel. On the other hand, they do not yet live in the transformed creation that was promised in connection with their restoration. They are at once restored and yet in some sense still in exile, living in a fallen world that is not their true home.

It is within this already/not-yet dynamic of restoration from exile while yet living as exiles in this fallen world that James's exhortations for living the Christian life should be understood. As E. Randolph Richards puts it, James addresses the question, "How do we live wisely during our brief remaining

---

(typically Jerusalem) consoles the assembled diaspora communities in the midst of their tribulation and admonishes them regarding their covenantal responsibilities in hope of the expected restoration." James M. Scott, "Jesus' Vision for the Restoration of Israel as the Basis for a Biblical Theology of the New Testament," in *Biblical Theology: Retrospect and Prospect*, ed. Scott J. Hafemann (Downers Grove, IL: InterVarsity Press, 2002), 141.

[8]Noted in Moo, *Letter of James*, 49. The *Testament of Benjamin* likely dates from the second century BC.

time in this exile?"[9] James's response, according to Richards, divides into two sections. In chapters 1–3, James draws on numerous wisdom motifs to call his readers to avoid the pitfalls that led to Israel's exile. In chapters 4–6, James uses numerous themes from Isaiah 58 to describe what life as a redeemed exile looks like in a fallen world. Life as a redeemed exile in a fallen world means:

- Fighting against the temptation to rebel against God (James 4:4; Isaiah 58:1)
- Not being a double-minded person (James 4:8; Isaiah 58:2-3)
- Drawing near to God (James 4:8; Isaiah 58:2)
- Pursuing humility (James 4:10; Isaiah 58:3)
- Not oppressing workers (James 5:4; Isaiah 58:3)
- Not using the Lord's time for personal business (James 4:13-15; Isaiah 58:3)
- Not quarreling and fighting (James 4:1; Isaiah 58:4)
- Caring for the poor and one's own family (James 5:13-20; Isaiah 58:7)
- Avoiding divisions that hinder answered prayer (James 4:11; Isaiah 58:9)
- Praying for God to heal the sick and restore sinners (James 5:15-20; Isaiah 58:8-14)[10]

As those who have been redeemed from their slavery to sin, God's people should live a life that demonstrates their eschatological restoration has already begun. Because we live in this fallen world, we still face the temptation to rebel against God and pursue friendship with this world rather than allow our lives to be shaped by our citizenship in heaven. As we humbly draw near to the God who brought us out of our exile from him, we will view ourselves as stewards of the possessions and time that God has given to us. Instead of devoting our energy to quarrelling with each other, we will pour out our lives to self-sacrificially love and care for those around us in need. Rather than speaking evil against each other, we will pray for God to bring relational,

---

[9] Pate et al., *Story of Israel*, 238.

[10] Adapted from material in Pate et al., *Story of Israel*, 240. Richards also notes a number of parallels between James and Leviticus 19:12-18, but is likely correct when he suggests these parallels are mediated through Isaiah 58.

physical, and spiritual healing. In all these ways and more, our lives now should reflect that our true home is not this fallen world but the new creation that God will consummate at the end of human history.

GALATIANS

In the previous chapter we saw that Paul portrays Jesus as the Suffering Servant who ends humanity's exile by bearing the curse for our disobedience (Galatians 3:10-14). Again in 4:1-7, Paul portrays our salvation in Christ as a new exodus out of our exile in this present evil age, which is under slavery to the elements of the world.[11] When Israel was in Egypt, they were slaves under Egyptian taskmasters ("guardians and managers") until the time appointed by the Father, even though they were heirs who legally owned everything (4:1-2). Their experience provides a pattern or type for the experience of all believers: "In the same way we also, when we were children, were in slavery under the elements of the world" (4:3 CSB).

Israel's Egyptian slavery is portrayed as a type of the greater slavery that humanity experienced under the elements of the world.[12] But just as God redeemed Israel at the appointed time, so too God has redeemed his people (Jew and Gentile alike) through an even greater redemptive act:

> But when the fullness of time had come, God sent forth his Son, born of woman, born under the law, to redeem those who were under the law, so that we might receive adoption as sons. And because you are sons, God has sent the Spirit of his Son into our hearts, crying, "Abba! Father!" So you are no longer a slave, but a son, and if a son, then an heir through God. (Galatians 4:4-7)

---

[11]For an extended reading of this passage through the lens of sin-exile-restoration, see Scott J. Hafemann, "Paul and the Exile of Israel in Galatians 3–4," in *Exile: Old Testament, Jewish, and Christian Conceptions*, ed. James M. Scott (Leiden, The Netherlands: Brill, 1997), 329-71. Ciampa sees in this passage the clearest example of the relationship between the two interlocking CSER structures, with Jesus resolving Israel's exile as the necessary first step in resolving humanity's exile. Roy E. Ciampa, "The History of Redemption," in *Central Themes in Biblical Theology: Mapping Unity in Diversity*, ed. Scott J. Hafemann and Paul R. House (Grand Rapids, MI: Baker Books, 2007), 300-301.

[12]The meaning of the expression "elements of the world" is widely debated. Most likely it refers to the basic elements of the material world. But Paul uses them to represent all that is associated with this fallen world, this present evil age (Galatians 1:4) that is under the curse that fell on creation as a result of Adam's rebellion.

God sent his Son to lead both Jews ("born under the law") and Gentiles ("born of woman") in a new exodus (note again the redemption language, using the same verb as in Galatians 3:13). By entering into this present evil age controlled by the elements of this world, the Son rescued his people from their slavery and granted them the status of adult sons. Instead of being children under the authority of the elements, believers are now adult sons who have been given the Spirit of God's Son. As a result, believers are heirs of the promises made to Abraham because they are in Christ, the promised seed of Abraham (3:16).

Paul returns to the sin-exile-restoration motif in 4:21–5:1, the climactic paragraph of his argument that all who believe in Jesus are fully justified sons of Abraham who inherit the promised blessing. Reading Genesis 16–21 through the lens of Isaiah 51–54, the apostle contrasts Hagar and the Mosaic law covenant (which operates on the basis of the flesh and produces sons who are enslaved) with Sarah and the Abrahamic covenant fulfilled in Christ (which operates on the basis of the promise and produces sons who are free). The former corresponds to the present Jerusalem, while the latter corresponds to the "Jerusalem above," which is the mother of believers. This last assertion is grounded in a citation of Isaiah 54:1: "For it is written, 'Rejoice, O barren one who does not bear; break forth and cry aloud, you who are not in labor! For the children of the desolate one will be more than those of the one who has a husband'" (Galatians 4:27).

In its original context, Isaiah 54:1 invites God's people to celebrate the servant redeeming them in fulfillment of the Abrahamic promise. The "Jerusalem above" is Paul's way of referring to the eschatological state that results from God fulfilling his promises to redeem his people from their sin, bring them out of their exile, and transform creation itself. Paul's point, then, is that through Jesus Christ's death on the cross and resurrection from the dead, he has brought into existence the eschatological people of God and inaugurated the promised new creation.

When Paul turns to describing the war between the flesh and the Spirit that the believer experiences (Galatians 5:16-26), he may also be drawing on return-from-exile motifs. In contrast to a life that is controlled by the desires of the flesh, Paul insists, "If you are led by the Spirit, you are not under the law" (5:18).

The language of being led by the Spirit may come from Isaiah 63:11-14, where the prophet invokes Yahweh's gracious presence among his people in the exodus as a type/pattern for God's even greater future presence among his people when he once again leads them in a second exodus.[13] Yet just as the Israelites in the wilderness were tempted to sinfully rebel against the Lord, so too believers face the very real danger of the works of the flesh (Galatians 5:19-21). Because believers live in the overlap between the inauguration of the new creation and the continuation of the present evil age, we experience the constant tug of the flesh enticing us to indulge sinful passions. The danger is so real that Paul insists anyone whose life is characterized by these works of the flesh will not inherit the kingdom of God when it is consummated.

But instead of lives dominated by the works of the flesh, believers are characterized by the fruit of the Spirit (Galatians 5:22-23). In describing this fruit, Paul appears to draw on two Isaianic texts (Isaiah 32:15-18; 57:15-19) that foretell a time when the Spirit will come from on high as part of God's eschatological salvation, producing fruit that is both physical in its transformation of the land and spiritual/moral in the transformation of his people. This pouring out of the Spirit is connected to the restoration of Israel and even more specifically that of Jerusalem. The fact that believers—Jew and Gentile—are led by and produce the fruit of the Spirit confirms that the era of eschatological fulfillment has begun.

For believers, the work of Christ, the suffering servant, has freed us from our slavery to sin, death, Satan, and all the evil powers associated with this present evil age. Through him believers are a people restored from their exile away from the presence of God and brought into his family as adopted sons. The defining evidence that they have inherited the blessing promised to Abraham is that they are now the place where the Spirit of God dwells. By walking in his power, we are able to live lives of obedience that bear the Spirit's fruit. Because we are in Christ, we already experience the peace and mercy that God had promised to his restored people as we await its consummation in a transformed creation.

---

[13]See William N. Wilder, *Echoes of the Exodus Narrative in the Context and Background of Galatians 5:18*, SBL 23 (New York: P. Lang, 2001), 130-38; and Matthew S. Harmon, *She Must and Shall Go Free: Paul's Isaianic Gospel in Galatians*, BZNW 168 (Berlin: de Gruyter, 2010), 221-25.

PHILIPPIANS

Although Philippians does not explicitly refer to Christians as exiles or sojourners, it is evident that Paul considers them to be such. Look, for example, how he states the central command of the letter: "As citizens of heaven, live your life worthy of the gospel of Christ" (Philippians 1:27 CSB).[14] Regardless of where believers physically live, they are citizens of God's kingdom. We live in this fallen world as exiles and sojourners whose primary allegiance is not to any earthly realm. During our pilgrimage in a place that is not our ultimate home, our lives are governed by "the gospel of Christ." Thus, the gospel is the constitution of God's kingdom that defines who we are and how we should live as God's people.

Given that our primary identity is citizens of a heavenly realm, believers should expect to suffer when our beliefs, values, and priorities conflict with those of this world (Philippians 1:27-30). Our common life together should instead reflect the self-sacrificial and humble love that our king Jesus Christ demonstrated through his death and resurrection (2:1-11). God empowers us to live out our identity as citizens of his kingdom, children of God who shine as lights in this sin-darkened world (2:12-18). He gives us examples of a Christlike life to demonstrate what it looks like to live as exiles who "press on toward the goal for the prize of the upward call of God in Christ Jesus" (2:19-3:14).

As he brings the body of the letter to a close, Paul again uses explicit citizenship language. However, he shifts from a focus on the present reality of that citizenship to the future when he writes, "Our citizenship is in heaven, and from it we await a Savior, the Lord Jesus Christ, who will transform our lowly body to be like his glorious body, by the power that enables him even to subject all things to himself" (Philippians 3:20-21).

As believers live out their heavenly citizenship, we are motivated by our hope that a day is coming when our Savior, Jesus Christ, returns from heaven.

---

[14]The Greek verb used here means to live as a citizen, but Paul does not explicitly indicate what kind of citizenship is in view. However, he does use the cognate noun in Philippians 3:20 to explicitly state, "our citizenship is in heaven." So the citizenship Paul refers to in 1:27 is also the believer's citizenship in heaven. For further discussion, see Matthew S. Harmon, *Philippians*, Mentor Commentary (Fearn, Ross-shire, Scotland: Christian Focus, 2015), 164-66.

As the one who obeyed where both Adam and Israel disobeyed, the risen
Jesus will complete the transformation of his people. He will resurrect our
bodies and complete our return from exile by settling us in a transformed
creation. At last we will be home.

CONCLUSION AND APPLICATION

Other passages could be explored, but the ones discussed above sufficiently
demonstrate our point.[15] Even though Jesus has inaugurated the end of our
exile, God's promises have not yet been consummated. Yes, we are the renewed
people of God, brought out of the exile that our sin caused. Yes, we as individuals and as a community are the beginning of the new creation, the place
where God dwells here on earth. Yes, God has seated us with Christ in the
heavenly places (Ephesians 2:6). Yes, we are children of the heavenly Jerusalem.
Yes, we experience God's presence in our lives to empower us to live as a
kingdom of priests who display the glory of our Creator. But there is still so
much more to come.

Even after the final New Testament document was written in the last
decade of the first century, believers recognized and embraced their identity
as exiles in this fallen world. Sometime in the second or third century, an
unknown Christian wrote a letter to a man named Diognetus. He appears to
have been curious about what Christians believed and how they lived. As
part of his answer, the author gives a lengthy explanation of how Christians
live in this world that is not their true home:

---

[15]For brief summaries of additional passages in Paul's writings, see Pate et al., *Story of Israel*, 206-31.
For passages in the general epistles, see Pate et al., *Story of Israel*, 232-54. Worth noting here is
Romans 5–8, which some have argued retells the story of Israel through the lens of Deuteronomic
history. See, e.g., Frank Thielman, "The Story of Israel and the Theology of Romans 5–8," in
Pauline Theology, ed. Jouette M. Bassler, David M. Hay, and E. Elizabeth Johnson (Minneapolis:
Fortress Press, 1991), 3:169-95; N. T. Wright, "New Exodus, New Inheritance: The Narrative
Substructure of Romans 3–8," in *Romans and the People of God: Essays in Honor of Gordon D. Fee
on the Occasion of His 65th Birthday*, ed. Sven Soderlund and N. T. Wright (Grand Rapids, MI:
Eerdmans, 1999), 26-35; Pate et al., *Story of Israel*, 214-17. For a helpful and concise response, see
Douglas J. Moo, "Israel and the Law in Romans 5–11: Interaction with the New Perspective," in
Justification and Variegated Nomism, vol. 2, *The Paradoxes of Paul*, ed. D. A. Carson, Peter T. O'Brien,
and Mark Seifrid (Grand Rapids, MI: Baker Books, 2004), 185-216. Moo concludes that while
there may be some echoes of these narratives in Romans 5–8, they remain in the background
and should not be used as a guide to interpret the development of the chapters.

They dwell in their own countries, but simply as sojourners. As citizens, they share in all things with others, and yet endure all things as if foreigners. Every foreign land is to them as their native country, and every land of their birth as a land of strangers. They marry, as do all [others]; they beget children; but they do not destroy their offspring. They have a common table, but not a common bed. They are in the flesh, but they do not live after the flesh. They pass their days on earth, but they are citizens of heaven. (*Epistle to Diognetus* 5:5-9)

That, in a nutshell, is the life of the Christian—as one who has been restored to fellowship with God through the work of Jesus yet still lives as an exile in this fallen world.

Unfortunately, we are not always aware of this tension, because our lives are comfortable. When we have a nice home, a job we really enjoy, meaningful relationships, financial security, and many of the other material blessings of this world, we can lose sight of the fact that this world is not truly our home. There is nothing inherently sinful about having those things, but when our enjoyment of them begins to blind us to our true identity as exiles and strangers, we are in danger of transforming those good gifts into idols that will turn our hearts away from God. If you go throughout your day and never feel any tension between your identity as a follower of Jesus and the world/culture around you, that is a dangerous signal that you have lost sight of our identity as exiles in a world that is not our home. You may even want to take a moment right now to ask the Lord to show you ways that you have become too comfortable in this fallen world.

We will not always live within this tension between the already and the not-yet. A day is coming when God will consummate his promises of restoration from exile in a new heavens and new earth. In the next chapter we will explore just how glorious that reality will be.

Chapter Eight

THE END OF EXILE CONSUMMATED IN A NEW CREATION

ONE MARK OF A GOOD STORY is that the ending corresponds to the beginning. We have all had the experience of watching a movie where the ending leaves us unsatisfied. Often it is because some element of the plot that was introduced early in the story was left hanging. When that happens, we tend to come away disappointed or frustrated, knowing that something is missing.

Thankfully the Bible is not that kind of story. Even a casual reading of Genesis 1–3 and Revelation 21–22 shows a lot of overlap. But there is more than simple overlap. The final two chapters of the Bible bring the story that begins in the first three chapters to its completion. The mission that God gave humanity is at last fulfilled and consummated. The problems of sin, death, and the serpent are decisively dealt with. God has at last eliminated the idolatry and rebellion that led to humanity being exiled from his presence. When this day finally comes, at last we will finally be home: God's people living in the place he has made for us and experiencing his presence. It is the ultimate "and they all lived happily ever after" story that makes all other such stories but pale shadows.

While there are several ways one could divide Revelation 21–22, we will do so through the lenses of the three different images that the apostle John uses to describe the consummated state of God's plan: a new heaven and earth, a new Jerusalem, and a new Eden.[1] As we look at each of these images, we will see the three key themes of people, place, and presence coming to their complete and final fullness. But before we can look at the final consummation of God's promises, we must first look at the final consummation of his judgment.

A FINAL EXILE (REVELATION 20:11-15)

Before God ushers in the final state of the new heavens and new earth, he must first execute final judgment on his enemies. John describes the scene like this:

> Then I saw a great white throne and him who was seated on it. From his presence earth and sky fled away, and no place was found for them. And I saw the dead, great and small, standing before the throne, and books were opened. Then another book was opened, which is the book of life. And the dead were judged by what was written in the books, according to what they had done. And the sea gave up the dead who were in it, Death and Hades gave up the dead who were in them, and they were judged, each one of them, according to what they had done. Then Death and Hades were thrown into the lake of fire. This is the second death, the lake of fire. And if anyone's name was not found written in the book of life, he was thrown into the lake of fire. (Revelation 20:11-15)

God summons the dead to appear before him to announce their final judgment. After Adam and Eve had sinned, God's presence had been cause for fear, and the same is true here. None of the dead are exempt from this

---

[1]Scholars debate how exactly these three images relate to one another. Some claim that they are simply three different images that portray the same reality (i.e., new heavens and earth = new Jerusalem = new Eden). Others see a progression that zooms in from the widest lens (new heavens and earth) to a medium-range lens (new Jerusalem) to a zoom lens (new Eden). Resolving the issue is not necessary for our purposes here.

final judgment, as it encompasses both great and small; even the sea, Death, and Hades are forced to give up their dead.

The judgment is carried out in accordance with what is written in the heavenly books, which highlights God's exhaustive knowledge of what each human being has done. This language echoes both Daniel 7:10 and 12:1-2; the first focuses on the evil works of those who persecute God's people, while the second focuses on the names of the righteous who will be resurrected to eternal life. Those whose names are not written in the book of life are cast in the lake of fire, where they will experience eternal torment for their sins (cf. Revelation 20:10).

Those who are tormented in the lake of fire experience the ultimate form of exile. They are cut off from God's people, who live in the place God has made for them—the fully consummated new creation (Revelation 21:8, 27). Because God is omnipresent, they are not completely cut off from God's presence; but rather than experience his presence as blessing, they experience it as judgment. They are separated from every aspect of God's goodness, kindness, mercy, and grace, leaving only the fiery torment of his holy wrath against sin. But in contrast to every other form of exile before, this time there is no hope of restoration. All that remains is the terrifying prospect of an eternity experiencing the curse that comes for rebellion against a holy God.

Such a horrifying picture brings into sharp relief the staggering nature of what God does to consummate his restoration promises in the new heavens and new earth.

A NEW HEAVEN AND A NEW EARTH
(REVELATION 21:1-8)

Let's start by looking at Revelation 21:1-4:

> Then I saw a new heaven and a new earth, for the first heaven and the first earth had passed away, and the sea was no more. And I saw the holy city, new Jerusalem, coming down out of heaven from God, prepared as a bride adorned for her husband. And I heard a loud voice from the throne saying, "Behold, the dwelling place of God is with man. He will dwell with them, and they will be his people, and God himself will be with them as their God. He will wipe away every tear from their eyes, and death shall be no more, neither

shall there be mourning, nor crying, nor pain anymore, for the former things have passed away."

The contrast between the new creation and the old creation is language drawn from Isaiah 65:17, where the old creation is further described as the "former things" that will no longer be remembered. This contrast between the former things and the new thing that God is doing to redeem his people from exile and transform creation runs as a steady current throughout Isaiah (42:9; 43:9, 18-21; 48:3; 65:16-17). The absence of the sea, commonly thought of in the ancient world as a source of chaos and evil, signals that in this new creation there is no longer even the possibility of a threat from Satan, the rebellious nations, or even death.[2] John introduces the New Jerusalem here as "a bride adorned for her husband," drawing language from Isaiah 52:1 and 61:10 that anticipated the fulfillment of God's promises to restore his people from exile. In this new creation, "the dwelling place of God is with man" (Revelation 21:3). The expression "dwelling place" is literally the word for tabernacle, which was God's temporary dwelling place with his people. That tabernacle (and eventually the temple that replaced it) were viewed as a microcosm of Eden, where God originally dwelled with his people. This language also echoes Ezekiel 43:7, which describes the eschatological temple that God promised would be his dwelling place.

John further signals that this new creation is the full realization of God's covenant promises by stating the covenant formula "they will be his people, and God himself will be with them as their God" (Revelation 21:3). Originally stated in Leviticus 26:11, it is repeated throughout the Old Testament. But most significantly it is stated in Ezekiel 37:28 and embedded in God's promise of a new covenant that he will institute with his people when he restores them from exile. Once God has consummated his promises, there will no longer be anything that produces grief (not even death!) in this new creation, just as God promised in Isaiah 25:8. Indeed, the former things—the realities of living in a fallen world marred by sin, the curse, Satan, and rebellious humanity—will truly pass away. The curse that God pronounced on creation because of Adam and Eve's rebellion will at last be reversed.

---

[2]See G. K. Beale, *The Book of Revelation: A Commentary on the Greek Text*, NIGTC (Grand Rapids, MI: Eerdmans, 1999), 1041-43, 50-51.

With the consummation of this new creation, God makes all things new. This expression echoes language from Isaiah 43:18-19, which refers to God transforming creation in fulfillment of his promise to bring his people out of their exile through a new exodus. God is able to make all things new because he is "the Alpha and the Omega, the beginning and the end" (Revelation 21:6; cf. Isaiah 44:6). Giving his thirsty people water to drink "from the spring of the water of life without payment" (Revelation 21:6) echoes the invitation of Isaiah 55:1-3, where God invites Jew and Gentile to enjoy the new covenant instituted by the work of the suffering servant in fulfillment of God's promises to David. This new creation is populated with those who have remained faithful to Christ even in the face of great tribulation, and because they are by faith united to Jesus Christ, the son of David, they too are sons of God (Revelation 21:7; cf. 2 Samuel 7:14). At last God's people are redeemed from their exile and live in a renewed land under a Davidic king, experiencing God's presence (cf. Ezekiel 37:24-28).

God had commissioned Adam to be fruitful and exercise dominion over the original creation. He made a garden where he dwelled with Adam and Eve. He had warned that the penalty for disobedience was death. When they disobeyed God at the prompting of the serpent, he cursed the original creation and sent humanity into exile from his presence. Yet he also promised a serpent-crusher who would obey where Adam failed and take on himself the curse for disobedience.

But now in this consummated creation brought about through the work of the last Adam, God's people have been redeemed from their exile. They are in the place where they ultimately belong. They experience God's presence in a way that even surpasses what Adam and Eve experienced in the garden.

A NEW JERUSALEM (REVELATION 21:9-27)

John now focuses his attention on the New Jerusalem, and his description falls into three distinct sections. The first is Revelation 21:9-14:

> Then came one of the seven angels who had the seven bowls full of the seven last plagues and spoke to me, saying, "Come, I will show you the Bride, the wife of the Lamb." And he carried me away in the Spirit to a great, high mountain, and showed me the holy city Jerusalem coming down out of

heaven from God, having the glory of God, its radiance like a most rare jewel, like a jasper, clear as crystal. It had a great, high wall, with twelve gates, and at the gates twelve angels, and on the gates the names of the twelve tribes of the sons of Israel were inscribed—on the east three gates, on the north three gates, on the south three gates, and on the west three gates. And the wall of the city had twelve foundations, and on them were the twelve names of the twelve apostles of the Lamb.

This opening section focuses on the stunning beauty and security of the New Jerusalem. At first this section may seem confusing, as the angel says to John that he will show him "the Bride, the wife of the Lamb" and then proceeds to show him "the holy city Jerusalem coming down out of heaven from God." But rather than an either-or, this is a both/and. The city refers to both God's people and the place where they dwell.[3]

Depicting God's redeemed and glorified people as a bride/wife further signals the consummation of his promise to restore them from exile. After exile, God had promised to betroth his people to himself forever in righteousness, justice, steadfast love, mercy, and faithfulness (Hosea 2:19-20). He had promised to clothe his redeemed people as a bride adorned with jewels (Isaiah 61:10). They would no longer be called forsaken and desolate, but rather

You shall be called My Delight Is in Her,
    and your land Married;
for the LORD delights in you,
    and your land shall be married.
For as a young man marries a young woman,
    so shall your sons marry you,
and as the bridegroom rejoices over the bride,
    so shall your God rejoice over you. (Isaiah 62:4-5)

With their sins completely dealt with and her enemies destroyed forever, the bride of the Lamb is now free to enjoy the consummation of her marriage to Christ.

---

[3]A similar dynamic is found in Galatians 4:26-27, where Paul refers to the "Jerusalem above" (i.e., the heavenly Jerusalem) as the mother of believers and grounds this claim in a citation of Isaiah 54:1.

The definitive characteristic of the city is that it has the glory of God, further described as the radiance of the rarest jasper. Just as Isaiah 58:8 and 60:1-2 had foreseen, the glory of God that was once restricted to the temple now permeates the entire city. The city's high walls and twelve gates stress that it is completely safe and secure; unlike the garden where the serpent was able to enter, the New Jerusalem will be completely secure from any and all enemies of God and his people. The twelve gates have the names of the twelve tribes of Israel, signaling that the promised restoration of the twelve tribes from their exile has at last been fully realized (Ezekiel 37:19; Hosea 1:11). Yet the twelve foundations of the city have the names of the twelve apostles. This glorified city is thus the home of God's people from both the Old and New Testaments, where they dwell together under the authority of their one Lord, Jesus Christ.

The second section, found in Revelation 21:15-21, focuses on the beauty and surpassing value of the city:

> And the one who spoke with me had a measuring rod of gold to measure the city and its gates and walls. The city lies foursquare, its length the same as its width. And he measured the city with his rod, 12,000 stadia. Its length and width and height are equal. He also measured its wall, 144 cubits by human measurement, which is also an angel's measurement. The wall was built of jasper, while the city was pure gold, like clear glass. The foundations of the wall of the city were adorned with every kind of jewel. The first was jasper, the second sapphire, the third agate, the fourth emerald, the fifth onyx, the sixth carnelian, the seventh chrysolite, the eighth beryl, the ninth topaz, the tenth chrysoprase, the eleventh jacinth, the twelfth amethyst. And the twelve gates were twelve pearls, each of the gates made of a single pearl, and the street of the city was pure gold, like transparent glass.

This description of the New Jerusalem is drawn primarily from Ezekiel 40–48, which portrays the eschatological temple that God would establish as the consummation of redeeming his people from exile. The angel uses his golden measuring rod (cf. Ezekiel 40:3-5) to show that the city is in fact a perfect cube: its length, width, and breadth are 12,000 stadia (or 1,380 miles).[4] As such, it is in fact the consummation of the temple itself, and more specifically

---

[4]A stadia was about 607 feet, so 12,000 stadia equals roughly 1,380 miles. But there is clearly a symbolic significance to 12,000; as Beale notes, "The equal measurement of twelve thousand stadia

the holy of holies, which was also in the shape of a cube (cf. 1 Kings 6:20). The New Jerusalem is now the consummated holy of holies, the place where God's manifest glory now dwells. With sin, death, and Satan finally put away forever, God's people are now able to dwell in the presence of God. Where the high priest could go only once a year after elaborate sacrificial and purification rituals (see Leviticus 16:1-34), God's redeemed people now live their everyday lives.

The walls of the city are also described in symbolic terms, with the wall measuring 144 cubits (or 200 feet). This emphasizes not only the security of the city but also its completeness, as 144 is twelve times twelve. The precious jewels that make up these walls echo the language of Exodus 28:17-20, where a similar list of jewels were placed in the high priest's breastplate that he wore. As such, they stood for the twelve tribes of Israel that the high priest represented when he entered God's presence. Additionally, John likely has Isaiah 54:11-12 in view, which describes the new Jerusalem that results from the suffering servant redeeming his people and restoring them from their exile.

The final section describing the New Jerusalem is Revelation 21:22-27:

> And I saw no temple in the city, for its temple is the Lord God the Almighty and the Lamb. And the city has no need of sun or moon to shine on it, for the glory of God gives it light, and its lamp is the Lamb. By its light will the nations walk, and the kings of the earth will bring their glory into it, and its gates will never be shut by day—and there will be no night there. They will bring into it the glory and the honor of the nations. But nothing unclean will ever enter it, nor anyone who does what is detestable or false, but only those who are written in the Lamb's book of life.

By stating that there is no temple in the city, John simply makes explicit what to this point has been implicit. There is no distinct structure that is the temple in the new creation, for all of the new creation is in fact the dwelling place of God, since he and the Lamb dwell there with his people in unhindered fellowship and fill this new creation with their presence.

---

of each of the city's four sides reinforces the figurative idea of the completeness of God's people found earlier in the mention of the twelve tribes and twelve apostles." *Book of Revelation*, 1073.

The remaining verses draw heavily from Isaiah 60, which again is set in the context of the consummated return from exile that God will accomplish through his suffering servant. Isaiah 60:19-20 describes how the sun and moon will be unnecessary to illuminate the new Jerusalem since God's glory will do so:

> The sun shall be no more
> your light by day,
> nor for brightness shall the moon
> give you light;
> but the LORD will be your everlasting light,
> and your God will be your glory.
> Your sun shall no more go down,
> nor your moon withdraw itself;
> for the LORD will be your everlasting light,
> and your days of mourning shall be ended.

That the gates of the New Jerusalem remain open for the nations to pour in further echoes Isaiah 60.[5] In the consummation, God had promised that the nations would bring gold and other precious gifts in praise to Yahweh (Isaiah 60:5-7). But Isaiah 60:11 is even more directly in view here: "Your gates shall be open continually; day and night they shall not be shut, that people may bring to you the wealth of the nations, with their kings led in procession."

The point here is not so much the physical wealth of the nations but rather the nations offering themselves as worshipers of God.[6] God has redeemed both Jews and Gentiles from their sin-imposed exile, and in the new creation he gathers them together to dwell among them.

A NEW EDEN (REVELATION 22:1-5)

The visions of this new creation culminates in a description of a new Eden, which John describes in Revelation 22:1-5:

---

[5]Note also Isaiah 35:6-8, which promises that when Israel returns from exile God will make a highway that leads straight to a renewed holy city of Zion. See Thomas R. Schreiner, "Revelation," in *ESV Expository Commentary*, vol. 12, *Hebrews-Revelation*, ed. Iain M. Duguid, James M. Hamilton, and Jay Sklar (Wheaton, IL: Crossway, 2018), 745.

[6]Beale, *Revelation*, 1095.

Then the angel showed me the river of the water of life, bright as crystal, flowing from the throne of God and of the Lamb through the middle of the street of the city; also, on either side of the river, the tree of life with its twelve kinds of fruit, yielding its fruit each month. The leaves of the tree were for the healing of the nations. No longer will there be anything accursed, but the throne of God and of the Lamb will be in it, and his servants will worship him. They will see his face, and his name will be on their foreheads. And night will be no more. They will need no light of lamp or sun, for the Lord God will be their light, and they will reign forever and ever.

The starting point in this description is the "river of the water of life." The original garden had a river that watered the land (Genesis 2:10-14), but the river here in the New Eden has an even greater significance: it provides the water of life. John continues to draw imagery from the description of the eschatological temple in Ezekiel 47:1-9, though the vision of waters flowing from a renewed Jerusalem in Zechariah 14:8 may also be in view as well. John may also have in mind Isaiah 35:6-9, which promised streams and springs of waters for the people God would redeem from their exile (cf. Isaiah 41:17-20; 43:18-20). Jesus had promised his people that all who believe in him would have rivers of living water flowing from their hearts, by which he meant the Holy Spirit (John 7:37-39). What believers experience in an inaugurated sense living in this fallen world will be experienced in the fullest sense in the New Eden. Regardless of whether the living waters in Revelation 22:1 are a symbolic representation of the Holy Spirit, the larger point is as clear as the crystal waters of the river of life. God is providing his people with an unending source of life that comes directly from himself.

In the original garden, Adam and Eve had been cut off from the Tree of Life after they sinned. But in the New Eden, God's redeemed people will have unfettered access to the Tree of Life and its twelve kinds of fruit that bring healing (cf. Ezekiel 47:8-12). In this new Eden there will be a complete and full realization of all God's redemptive purposes. The healing miracles Jesus performed during his earthly ministry were an anticipation of the final healing pictured here in the new Eden, and it is available to those from every nation who have trusted in Jesus Christ, the last Adam.

Although it should be obvious at this point, John wants to ensure that we do not miss the point that "no longer will there be anything accursed." Zechariah 14:11 had foreseen a day when a restored Jerusalem would never again be subject to a divine decree of utter destruction for her sin, and that is what has now come to pass in the New Eden. The curse that came on creation when Adam rebelled and resulted in their exile from the garden—gone! The curse that fell on Israel for failing to keep God's covenant and resulted in exile from the land—gone! The curse that falls on all who rely on the works of the law and results in exile away from God's presence—gone! The curse that rested on all humanity for their rebellion against God as sons of Adam and resulted in humanity's exile away from the presence of God—gone! All because Christ as the suffering servant became a curse for his people, taking on himself the exile that we deserved and rising from the dead as the firstborn of God's new creation who leads us out of exile into the very presence of God.

Because there is no hint of anything accursed, God is now able to dwell with his people in the fullness of his glory, power, and holiness. His throne that had once been exalted in the heavens (Hebrews 9:11-12; Revelation 4:1–5:14) has now come down to rest in this renewed creation. God had created the original Eden to be his sanctuary on his earth, but in this new Eden God's immediate and glorious presence fills every inch of the new creation, such that the promise that "the earth shall be full of the knowledge of the LORD as the waters cover the sea" (Isaiah 11:9; cf. Habakkuk 2:14) is now completely fulfilled.

With the curse finally gone and God's glorious presence filling the new creation, humanity is at last able to live out our true purpose as image-bearers: "his servants will serve him." The verb translated "serve" has the sense of serving as a priest. God's redeemed people are thus priests serving the Lord in this new creation sanctuary. They are able to live out the priestly commission that God gave to Adam but failed to fulfill. God had promised that when he brought his people back from their exile, all of them would be called "priests of the LORD" (Isaiah 61:6), and that comes to fruition in the new Eden. As our great high priest (Hebrews 4:14–5:9; 7:1–10:18), Jesus Christ the suffering servant gave his life as an offering (Isaiah 52:13–53:12), and in doing so he created a servant people.

With every last remnant of sin, the curse, and the serpent absent from this new Eden, God's people will at last see his face. Whereas in the original Eden God walked with Adam and Eve in the cool of the day, in the new Eden God's redeemed people will see his face, something that even saints like Moses and David longed for but never experienced (Exodus 33:20; Psalm 27:4). Believers living in this fallen world have seen a glimpse of the face of Christ (2 Corinthians 4:6) but must pursue holiness in anticipation of the day when they will see Christ face to face (1 John 3:2-3). Since all of God's renewed people are priests in the new Eden, they will have God's name written on their foreheads, just as the high priest did under the old covenant (Exodus 39:30-31). The promise of a new name given to his people after their return from exile will at last come to pass (Isaiah 62:2; 65:15).

After once again noting the lack of night and the continual illumination of the new creation by God himself, the description of the New Eden concludes by stating that God's renewed people "will reign forever and ever." At last the dominion over creation that God commissioned Adam to execute will come to its complete and full realization (Genesis 1:28). As the last Adam, Jesus Christ overcomes all the enemies of God's people, making them free to exercise the royal authority that God designed humanity to have under the ultimate authority of the Lamb who was slain.

Perhaps even more clearly than in any other part of Revelation 21–22 we see in this section the full consummation of God's purposes. God's people (Jew and Gentile alike) have been renewed and marked off as kings and priests. God has given the ultimate place to dwell: a new Eden that far exceeds even the glory of the original Eden. And most significantly, God's people now experience the fullness of God's presence as they see him face to face.

CONCLUSION AND APPLICATION

At last God's people are truly home—free from every last stain of sin, the curse, sickness, death, and even Satan himself. Unending joy in the presence of God forever is the promise that Revelation 21–22 holds out for those who have put their trust in Jesus: all of God's people living together in the place he has made for us, enjoying his presence forever. Only then will we as human beings be able to live out fully our purpose as image bearers. What seems to be too good to be true will one day be a reality. John Newton summarized it well in his hymn "Amazing Grace":

> When we've been there, ten thousand years,
> Bright shining as the sun
> We've no less days to sing God's praise
> Than when we'd first begun

As believers, our hope is not in anything this world offers. At their best, the things of this world are merely shadows of greater realities in the new creation. Even at their best, these shadows can never fully satisfy. Because our hope is the glorious appearing of the Lord Jesus (Titus 2:13), we must pursue a life of purity in the present as we wait for him to return for his people (1 John 3:1-3). When at last we see the risen and glorious Jesus Christ, the sufferings of this world will pale in comparison to the glories we will experience (Romans 8:18).

Chapter Nine

THE PRACTICAL IMPLICATIONS OF SIN, EXILE, AND RESTORATION

HOME AT LAST. A place where we truly belong. A place where we are truly free to be who we were made to be. A place that defines who we are. A place that transcends even the best this fallen world can offer. That is the new creation. That is our true home as God's people.

The biblical story begins with God placing Adam and his wife, Eve, in a garden to rule over creation. It ends with the last Adam, Jesus Christ, and his bride, the church, in a new garden ruling over a new creation. The sin that brought about humanity's exile from God's presence has been decisively done away with once and for all through the work of Jesus, who took the curse that we deserved. Through his resurrection from the dead, Jesus leads his people out of their exile and pours out the Spirit to dwell in his people. As his people redeemed from our spiritual exile, we announce this good news to the world in anticipation of the day when he transforms all of creation.

No wonder, then, it is possible to experience *Fernweh*—a homesickness for a place we have never visited. That's because we as human beings were made for a place where the unfulfilled longings we experience in this fallen world will at last be fulfilled.

Can you even begin to imagine what that will be like?

It sounds too good to be true, doesn't it? Like a fairy tale where the hero saves the princess in danger and everyone lives happily ever after.

But the story of the Bible is no fairy tale. It is the true story of the world, the true story from which every other story finds its meaning and significance. And it is the story that makes sense of everything we experience in this fallen world. Our lives are not ultimately a meaningless collection of events and relationships. God created us for a specific purpose that far transcends the limited scope of our individual lives.

As the previous chapters have shown, biblical theology is far from a merely academic exercise. It has direct and significant application to our everyday lives as the people of God. Tracing the thread of sin and exile through the Bible helps us to live as God intended us to live in this fallen world. Let's reflect on seven specific payoffs from our study of this important theme.

First, it enables us to understand who God is and his plan for this world. As A. W. Tozer famously wrote, "What comes into our minds when we think about God is the most important thing about us."[1] God is the central character of the biblical story. Even when he is not explicitly mentioned, he is clearly the one at work behind the scenes, sovereignly orchestrating events and raising up people to accomplish his purposes for this world. As we have traced the sin-exile theme, the fullness of God's character has been on display. His power is clearly seen not only in creating the world but perhaps even more clearly in his numerous redemptive acts (with particular emphasis on Israel's exodus from Egypt and the new exodus that Jesus accomplishes for his people through his death and resurrection). His people sin, God sends them into exile, but he eventually brings them back to himself.

But perhaps the most noticeable attribute of God that emerges from studying the sin-exile theme is the stunning grace and mercy of God in the face of humanity's persistent rebellion and failures. It begins with the promise

[1] A. W. Tozer, *The Knowledge of the Holy*, 1st HarperCollins gift ed. (New York: HarperSanFrancisco, 1992), 1.

of a serpent-crusher in the immediate aftermath of Adam's failure. When Israel sins by creating the golden calf, God reveals to Moses what is at the heart of the meaning of his name Yahweh (i.e., the Lord):

> The LORD, the LORD, a God merciful and gracious, slow to anger, and abounding in steadfast love and faithfulness, keeping steadfast love for thousands, forgiving iniquity and transgression and sin, but who will by no means clear the guilty, visiting the iniquity of the fathers on the children and the children's children, to the third and the fourth generation. (Exodus 34:6-7)

Mercy and grace are at the heart of who God is. Without in any way compromising his justice, God delights to show mercy and grace to his people. Far from being reluctant to forgive, Yahweh shows time and time again that he is eager to do so. Even though he knows his people will rebel against him and be sent into exile, God repeatedly promises to have mercy on them and restore them. And when he fulfills these promises in Jesus, he does so because of his steadfast love for his people. No matter how far you may feel from God, you are never beyond the reach of his mercy and grace shown through Jesus. When we truly see the staggering mercy and grace of God shown to us preeminently in the cross, we cannot remain the same.

Second, it enables us to understand who we are as human beings. In the opening lines of his famous work *Institutes of the Christian Religion*, John Calvin observed that "it is certain that man never achieves a clear knowledge of himself unless he has first looked upon God's face, and then descends from contemplating him to scrutinize himself."[2] To be human is to be an image bearer. We were made to reflect his glory. God crowned us to rule over creation and commissioned us to mediate his presence to this world. He set us apart from the rest of creation and made us to live in community with each other.

That is our identity as human beings. That is who God made us to be. The world tells us a different story. It tells us that we are nothing more than a collection of cells, the product of a long, impersonal evolutionary process. It tells us the only meaning to this life is what we make of it ourselves. But the

---

[2]John Calvin, *Institutes of the Christian Religion*, trans. John T. McNeill (Philadelphia: Westminster Press, 1960), 1:38.

Bible shows us who we truly are, and that is the first step to living as we were made to live.

Third, it enables us to understand what is wrong with this world. Anyone paying attention can see that this world is messed up. And if we are honest with ourselves, so are we as human beings. Only the Bible gives us a clear and satisfactory answer as to why the world is the way that it is. Sin entered the world through our first parents, Adam and Eve. As their descendants, we not only experience the consequences of their disobedience but also inherit their bent toward sin. By default, we come into this world as rebels against God, who naturally pursue our own selfish agendas and seek to live autonomously from God. Instead of exercising dominion over creation under the authority of God, we seek to do our own thing our own way based on our own desires. Instead of worshiping the God who created us, we commit idolatry by worshiping what God created, even ourselves.

And as we have so regularly seen through the Bible, the result of that rebellion and idolatry is exile away from the presence of God. At the root of what is wrong with this world is our distance from God. As our Creator, he is the source of everything good in this world, even in its cursed state. Our greatest need as human beings is to be reconciled to a holy God and brought into his presence.

Fourth, it enables us to understand what God has done to fix this broken world through Jesus. We as human beings may have been the ones that broke the good world that God originally made, but it must be God who fixes it. Even in the midst of bringing necessary judgment for Adam and Eve's rebellion, God promised a serpent-crusher from Eve who would obey where Adam had failed and take on himself the punishment for Adam's failure. Through his covenant with Abraham, God works to bring this promised serpent-crusher into the world to bring humanity out of its exile. He forms Abraham's descendants into the nation of Israel. Yet as God's people waited for this promised one, they regularly sinned and experienced exile away from the presence of God. When Jesus comes into the world as the serpent-crusher, he obeys where Adam, Israel, and every single one of us had disobeyed. He takes on himself the curse that we deserved for our rebellion and idolatry, willingly going into exile away from the Father's presence through his death on the cross.

Three days later he rises from the dead to lead his people out of their exile away from God and into the promised new creation. He pours out his Spirit on his people. Through his indwelling Spirit, God progressively works to restore his marred image in us so that we can live as he intended us to live.

Fifth, it enables us to understand that this world is not our true home. Throughout history, God's people have often been painfully aware that this present world is not our true home. Pain and suffering in this present world are two of the instruments God uses to remind us that even though Christ has rescued us from our spiritual exile from God, we continue to live in this fallen world as exiles and strangers. We are a pilgrim people, called to seek the ultimate good of those around us while recognizing that we are simply passing through on our way to our true home—the new creation.

Yet for Christians who live in places where there is little to no suffering and abundant comfort, it can be easy to forget this reality. We can be tempted to invest all of our time, energy, and resources into building and protecting a comfortable existence for ourselves. Remembering our status as redeemed exiles enables us to recognize the idol of comfort and order our lives for the advancement of God's kingdom rather than the protection of our own comfort.

Sixth, it enables us to understand how to live as God's people in this fallen world. Embracing that we are exiles and strangers in this world establishes a paradigm for us to view our everyday lives. Lee Beach may be right when he states that "the recovery of an exilic paradigm as a means of self-definition is absolutely necessary for the church in postmodern, post-Christian times."[3] God has not simply redeemed us as individuals; he has saved us into a community of people that he calls the church. That is where as believers we will find our true sense of belonging, all the while recognizing that as long as we live in this present evil age, sin will still affect even these

---

[3]Lee Beach, *The Church in Exile: Living in Hope After Christendom* (Downers Grove, IL: InterVarsity Press, 2015), 20. In this he follows Walter Brueggemann, *Cadences of Home: Preaching Among Exiles*, 1st ed. (Louisville, KY: Westminster John Knox, 1997) and Walter Brueggemann and Patrick D. Miller, *Deep Memory, Exuberant Hope: Contested Truth in a Post-Christian World* (Minneapolis: Fortress Press, 2000). Of course, seeing the experience of the church through the lens of exile goes back to at least the time of the Reformation, when Martin Luther famously described the true church as living in a Babylonian exile under the oppression of the Roman Catholic Church. See Martin Luther, Erik H. Herrmann, and Paul W. Robinson, *The Babylonian Captivity of the Church, 1520*, Annotated Luther Study Edition (Minneapolis: Fortress Press, 2016).

relationships. Living in community with fellow believers also enables us to work together to live as image bearers who live as kings and priests in this fallen world. As we do so, we experience the freedom that comes from living as God intended us to live.

Our common life together as people who have been redeemed out of our spiritual exile enables us to live as an outpost of God's kingdom in this fallen world. As the church, we are called to be ambassadors of Christ who announce the good news that anyone who trusts in him can be brought out of their spiritual exile from God. We make that restoration from exile visible as the church when we welcome the outcast and the marginalized and love those on the fringes of society.

Seventh, it enables us to understand where our true hope lies. Even as believers we can begin to set our hope for realities in this life that cannot ultimately deliver. We think that if we just get the right spouse, the right job, the right house, or the right income we will finally be happy and fulfilled. Or maybe we put our hopes in the political process, thinking that if we just get the right candidates into office everything will work out. The world around us is desperately looking for someone or something reliable to put their hope in.

The Bible reminds us in no uncertain terms that our ultimate hope rests not in improving our circumstances in this world but in God bringing a new creation. It is that hope that reminds us who we really are and gives us motivation to live for God's glory in this fallen world. Paul captures this reality beautifully in Romans 8:18-25:

> For I consider that the sufferings of this present time are not worth comparing with the glory that is to be revealed to us. For the creation waits with eager longing for the revealing of the sons of God. For the creation was subjected to futility, not willingly, but because of him who subjected it, in hope that the creation itself will be set free from its bondage to corruption and obtain the freedom of the glory of the children of God. For we know that the whole creation has been groaning together in the pains of childbirth until now. And not only the creation, but we ourselves, who have the firstfruits of the Spirit, groan inwardly as we wait eagerly for adoption as sons, the redemption of our bodies. For in this hope we were saved. Now hope that is seen is not

hope. For who hopes for what he sees? But if we hope for what we do not see, we wait for it with patience.

Suffering now with glory incomparable yet to come, groaning along with creation in anticipation of our bodily resurrection, waiting with eager anticipation and patience for the consummation of all God's promises in a new creation—that is our unshakable and glorious hope.

Not only is that our hope; it's the message that God sends us out into this fallen world to proclaim and authenticate through our transformed lives. Through the work of Jesus, God has made us into a people. He has made us the place where he dwells in anticipation of living with us in the new heavens and new earth. He has given us his presence to be with us to the end of age until we see him face to face in the new creation. That is the good news of the gospel that we are called to believe, live out, and proclaim in anticipation of Jesus' return to consummate his promises.

RECOMMENDATIONS FOR FURTHER READING

THE THEME OF EXILE has received a good bit of attention in scholarly circles, though less so in more popular-level writings. Arguably, the most significant catalyst for this attention has been the work of N. T. Wright, who argues that "return from exile" is the central motif for understanding the life, ministry, death, and resurrection of Jesus. His prolific writings have provoked a significant response from a variety of scholars, with varying levels of agreement and disagreement.

For those who may be interested in pursuing this theme of sin-exile-restoration, the following books and essays are a good place to start. This list is by no means exhaustive but rather is representative and broken down into three categories (beginner, intermediate, advanced). Within each category the works are listed in alphabetical order. For each work I have tried to give a brief description to help orient the reader.

BEGINNER

Lee Beach. *The Church in Exile: Living in Hope After Christendom.* Downers Grove, IL: InterVarsity Press, 2015.

Written for a broad audience, this book explains the value of the theme of
exile as a framework for the church in the West. After exploring selected
portions of Scripture that deal with the theme of exile, Beach sketches a vision
for how the church embracing its identity as a community of exiles would
enhance its holiness, mission, and hope.

**Iain M. Duguid. "Exile." In *New Dictionary of Biblical Theology*, edited
by T. Desmond Alexander and Brian S. Rosner, 475-78. Downers Grove,
IL: InterVarsity Press, 2000.**

A concise summary of the exile theme and the places where it is most prominent in Scripture. An excellent starting point for getting an initial grasp of
this theme.

INTERMEDIATE

**Stephen G. Dempster. *Dominion and Dynasty: A Biblical Theology of the
Hebrew Bible*. New Studies in Biblical Theology. Downers Grove, IL:
InterVarsity Press, 2003.**

Although not specifically focused on the theme of sin-exile, this book is one
of the most helpful for understanding the story line of the Old Testament.
Taking his cues from the structure of the Hebrew Bible, Dempster demonstrates the centrality of the promises of land and line embedded within the
Abrahamic promise as the key to the Old Testament metanarrative.

**C. Marvin Pate, et al. *The Story of Israel: A Biblical Theology*. Downers
Grove, IL: InterVarsity Press, 2004.**

Arguing that the sin-exile-restoration pattern evident in Israel's story is a
microcosm of humanity's universal story, this book surveys each major section
of the Bible through this lens. While acknowledging a diversity of emphases
in each section of the Bible, the various authors helpfully demonstrate the
value of this theme for seeing unity across the biblical story line.

ADVANCED

**Roy Ciampa, "History of Redemption." In *Central Themes in Biblical
Theology: Mapping Unity in Diversity*, edited by Scott J. Hafemann and
Paul R. House, 254-308. Grand Rapids, MI: Baker Books, 2007.**

In this lengthy essay, Ciampa presents the entire story line of the Bible in terms of the pattern of covenant-sin-exile-restoration (CSER). He argues that the Old Testament contains two interlocking CSER structures: a global one involving all humanity and a national one centered on Israel. Ciampa argues that understanding the relationship between the two interlocking CSER structures is crucial for understanding God's kingdom promises and purposes.

Carey C. Newman, ed. *Jesus and the Restoration of Israel: A Critical Assessment of N. T. Wright's Jesus and the Victory of God.* **Downers Grove, IL: InterVarsity Press, 1999.**

Twelve scholars from a variety of disciplines and viewpoints interact with N. T. Wright's proposal that return from exile is the key framework for understanding the life, ministry, death, and resurrection of Jesus. As you would expect, there are varying degrees of appreciation and disagreement. This volume includes Wright's response to the various critiques raised in the book.

Brant J. Pitre. *Jesus, the Tribulation, and the End of the Exile: Restoration Eschatology and the Origin of the Atonement.* **WUNT 2/204. Tübingen, Germany: Mohr Siebeck, 2005.**

Pitre explores the interlocking relationship between tribulation, Israel's restoration from exile, and the work of the Messiah. After an exploration of these themes in Second Temple Judaism, Pitre engages in a detailed study of the Gospels for these same themes. He concludes that Jesus understood himself to be setting into motion the Great Tribulation that would inaugurate the regathering of Israel from exile and the coming kingdom of God, with his own death playing a redemptive role in that restoration.

James M. Scott, ed. *Exile: A Conversation with N. T. Wright.* **Downers Grove, IL: InterVarsity Press, 2017.**

Similar to the volume edited by Carey Newman, this book contains essays from twelve different scholars from a variety of disciplines engaging N. T. Wright's work on exile. Especially helpful are Wright's introductory essay summarizing his view and his concluding essay responding to the various critiques raised in the volume.

James M. Scott, ed. *Exile: Old Testament, Jewish, and Christian Conceptions.* JSNTSup 56. New York: Brill, 1997.

This technical volume explores the exile theme in Jewish and Christian literature during key periods (Babylonian and Persian, Greco-Roman, Formative Judaism, and Early Christianity). For those interested in exploring the primary sources, this volume is a good place to begin.

James M. Scott, "Jesus' Vision for the Restoration of Israel as the Basis for a Biblical Theology of the New Testament." In *Biblical Theology: Retrospect and Prospect*, edited by Scott J. Hafemann, 129-43. Downers Grove, IL: InterVarsity Press, 2002.

In this shorter essay, Scott contends that the life, ministry, death, and resurrection of Jesus are best understood through the lens of Jesus restoring Israel. Even the Gentile mission of the early church is seen as a reflection of numerous Old Testament passages that envisioned the nations participating in Israel's restoration from exile.

N. T. Wright. *Christian Origins and the Question of God.* Vol. 1, *The New Testament and the People of God.* Minneapolis: Fortress Press, 1992.

N. T. Wright. *Christian Origins and the Question of God.* Vol. 2, *Jesus and the Victory of God.* Minneapolis: Fortress Press, 1996.

N. T. Wright. *Christian Origins and the Question of God.* Vol. 3, *The Resurrection of the Son of God.* Minneapolis: Fortress Press, 2003.

Regardless of whether one agrees with Wright, no one can dispute the significance of his work. He contends that the primary framework for understanding the life, ministry, death, and resurrection of Jesus is the conviction that first-century Jews believed that Israel's exile had not ended. Jesus understood himself to be an eschatological prophet who through his various actions (culminating in his death and resurrection) was bringing that exile to an end.

BIBLIOGRAPHY

Alexander, T. Desmond. *From Paradise to the Promised Land: An Introduction to the Pentateuch*. 2nd ed. Grand Rapids, MI: Baker Books, 2002.

———. "Further Observations on the Term 'Seed' in Genesis." *Tyndale Bulletin* 48 (1997): 363-67.

Alexander, T. Desmond and Brian S. Rosner, eds. *New Dictionary of Biblical Theology*. Leicester, England: InterVarsity Press, 2000.

Augustine. *The City of God*. In vol. 2 of *The Nicene and Post-Nicene Fathers*, Series 1. Edited by Philip Schaff. 1886-1889. 14 vols. Repr. Grand Rapids, MI: Eerdmans, 1952.

Beach, Lee. *The Church in Exile: Living in Hope After Christendom*. Downers Grove, IL: InterVarsity Press, 2015.

Beale, G. K. *The Book of Revelation: A Commentary on the Greek Text*. New International Greek Testament Commentary. Grand Rapids, MI: Eerdmans, 1999.

———. *A New Testament Biblical Theology: The Unfolding of the Old Testament in the New*. Grand Rapids, MI: Baker Books, 2011.

———. "The Old Testament Background of Reconciliation in 2 Corinthians 5–7 and Its Bearing on the Literary Problem of 2 Corinthians 6:14–7:1." In *Right Doctrine from the Wrong Texts? Essays on the Use of the Old Testament in the New*, edited by G. K. Beale, 217-47. Grand Rapids, MI: Baker Books, 1994.

———. "Peace and Mercy upon the Israel of God." *Biblica* 80 (1999): 204-23.

———. *The Temple and the Church's Mission: A Biblical Theology of the Dwelling Place of God*. New Studies in Biblical Theology 17. Downers Grove, IL: InterVarsity Press, 2004.

Blackburn, W. Ross. *The God Who Makes Himself Known: The Missionary Heart of the Book of Exodus*. New Studies in Biblical Theology 28. Downers Grove, IL: InterVarsity Press, 2012.

Brueggemann, Walter. *Cadences of Home: Preaching Among Exiles.* 1st ed. Louisville, KY: Westminster John Knox Press, 1997.

Brueggemann, Walter, and Patrick D. Miller. *Deep Memory, Exuberant Hope: Contested Truth in a Post-Christian World.* Minneapolis: Fortress Press, 2000.

Calvin, John. *Institutes of the Christian Religion.* Translated by John T. McNeill. Philadelphia: Westminster Press, 1960.

Carson, D. A. "Matthew." In *The Expositor's Bible Commentary,* edited by Frank E. Gaebelein, 1-492. Grand Rapids, MI: Zondervan, 1994.

Ceresko, Anthony R. "The Rhetorical Strategy of the Fourth Servant Song (Isaiah 52:13–53:12): Poetry and the Exodus-New Exodus." *Catholic Biblical Quarterly* 56 (1994): 42-55.

Chesterton, G. K. *As I Was Saying: A Chesterton Reader.* Grand Rapids, MI: Eerdmans, 1985.

Christensen, Duane L. *Deuteronomy 21:10–34:12.* Word Biblical Commentary 6B. Nashville: Thomas Nelson, 2002.

Ciampa, Roy E. "The History of Redemption." In *Central Themes in Biblical Theology: Mapping Unity in Diversity,* edited by Scott J. Hafemann and Paul R. House, 254-308. Grand Rapids, MI: Baker Books, 2007.

Collins, C. John. *Did Adam and Eve Really Exist? Who They Were and Why You Should Care.* Wheaton, IL: Crossway, 2011.

Craigie, Peter C. *The Book of Deuteronomy.* New International Commentary on the Old Testament. Grand Rapids, MI: Eerdmans, 1976.

Davies, W. D., and Dale C. Allison. *A Critical and Exegetical Commentary on the Gospel According to Saint Matthew.* 3 vols. International Critical Commentary. New York: T&T Clark International, 2004.

Dempster, Stephen G. *Dominion and Dynasty: A Biblical Theology of the Hebrew Bible.* New Studies in Biblical Theology 15. Downers Grove, IL: InterVarsity Press, 2003.

Dickens, Charles. *A Tale of Two Cities.* Philadelphia: Courage Books, 1992.

Dumbrell, William J. *Covenant and Creation: An Old Testament Covenantal Theology.* Rev. ed. Exeter, Devon, UK: Paternoster, 2013.

Evans, Craig A. "Aspects of Exile and Restoration in the Proclamation of Jesus and the Gospels." In Scott, *Exile: Old Testament,* 299-328.

Frost, Michael. *Exiles: Living Missionally in a Post-Christian Culture.* Peabody, MA: Hendrickson, 2006.

Garrett, Duane A. *Hosea, Joel.* New American Commentary 19A. Nashville: Broadman & Holman, 1997.

Gentry, Peter J., and Stephen J. Wellum. *Kingdom Through Covenant: A Biblical-Theological Understanding of the Covenants.* Wheaton, IL: Crossway, 2012.

Gladd, Benjamin L., and Matthew S. Harmon. *Making All Things New: Inaugurated Eschatology for the Life of the Church*. Grand Rapids, MI: Baker Books, 2016.

Goldingay, John. *Old Testament Theology*. Vol. 1, *Israel's Gospel*. Downers Grove, IL: InterVarsity Press, 2003.

Grundhauser, Eric. "Have You Ever Felt Homesick for a Place You've Never Been?" Atlas Obscura, February 27, 2018, www.atlasobscura.com/articles/homesick-for-place -you-have-never-been.

Guelich, Robert A. "Matthean Beatitudes: 'Entrance-Requirements' or Eschatological Blessings?" *Journal of Biblical Literature* 95 (1976): 415-34.

Hafemann, Scott J. "Paul and the Exile of Israel in Galatians 3–4." In Scott, *Exile: Old Testament*, 329-71.

Harmon, Matthew S. *Philippians*. Mentor Commentary. Fearn, Ross-shire, Scotland: Christian Focus, 2015.

———. *She Must and Shall Go Free: Paul's Isaianic Gospel in Galatians*. Beihefte zur Zeitschrift für die neutestamentliche Wissenschaft und die Kunde der älteren Kirche 168. Berlin: de Gruyter, 2010.

Horton, Michael S. *The Christian Faith: A Systematic Theology for Pilgrims on the Way*. Grand Rapids, MI: Zondervan, 2010.

House, Paul R. "Sin in the Law." In *Fallen: A Theology of Sin*, edited by Christopher W. Morgan and Robert A. Peterson, 39-63. Wheaton, IL: Crossway, 2013.

Hugenberger, G. P. "The Servant of the Lord in the 'Servant Songs' of Isaiah: A Second Moses Figure." In *The Lord's Anointed: Interpretation of Old Testament Messianic Texts*, edited by P. E. Satterthwaite, Richard S. Hess, and Gordon J. Wenham, 105-39. Grand Rapids, MI: Baker Books, 1995.

Janowski, Bernd, and Peter Stuhlmacher, eds. *The Suffering Servant: Isaiah 53 in Jewish and Christian Sources*. Grand Rapids, MI: Eerdmans, 2004.

Kline, Meredith G. *Kingdom Prologue: Genesis Foundations for a Covenantal Worldview*. Overland Park, KS: Two Age Press, 2000.

Knibb, Michael A. "Exile in the Damascus Document." *Journal for the Study of the Old Testament* 25 (1983): 99-117.

———. "The Exile in the Intertestamental Period." *Heythrop Journal* 18 (1977): 253-72.

Lane, William L. *The Gospel According to Mark*. New International Commentary on the New Testament. Grand Rapids, MI: Eerdmans, 1974.

Lewis, C. S. *Mere Christianity*. New York: HarperOne, 2001.

Lints, Richard. *Identity and Idolatry: The Image of God and Its Inversion*. New Studies in Biblical Theology 36. Downers Grove, IL: InterVarsity Press, 2015.

Luther, Martin, Erik H. Herrmann, and Paul W. Robinson. *The Babylonian Captivity of the Church, 1520*. The Annotated Luther Study Edition. Minneapolis: Fortress Press, 2016.

Martin, Oren R. *Bound for the Promised Land: The Land Promise in God's Redemptive Plan*. New Studies in Biblical Theology 34. Downers Grove, IL: InterVarsity Press, 2015.

McKnight, Scot. *The King Jesus Gospel: The Original Good News Revisited*. Grand Rapids, MI: Zondervan, 2011.

Merrill, Eugene H. *Deuteronomy*. New American Commentary 4. Nashville: Broadman & Holman, 1994.

Moo, Douglas J. "Israel and the Law in Romans 5–11: Interaction with the New Perspective." In *Justification and Variegated Nomism*. Vol. 2, *The Paradoxes of Paul*, edited by D. A. Carson, Peter T. O'Brien, and Mark Seifrid, 185-216. Grand Rapids, MI: Baker Books, 2004.

———. *The Letter of James*. Pillar New Testament Commentary. Grand Rapids, MI: Eerdmans, 2000.

Morales, L. Michael. *Who Shall Ascend the Mountain of the Lord? A Biblical Theology of the Book of Leviticus*. New Studies in Biblical Theology 37. Downers Grove, IL: InterVarsity Press, 2015.

Newman, Carey C., ed. *Jesus and the Restoration of Israel: A Critical Assessment of N. T. Wright's Jesus and the Victory of God*. Downers Grove, IL: InterVarsity Press, 1999.

Pao, David W. *Acts and the Isaianic New Exodus*. Biblical Studies Library. Grand Rapids, MI: Baker Books, 2002.

Pate, C. Marvin, J. Scott Duvall, J. Daniel Hays, E. Randolph Richards, W. Dennis Tucker Jr., and Preben Vang. *The Story of Israel: A Biblical Theology*. Downers Grove, IL: InterVarsity Press, 2004.

Pitre, Brant J. *Jesus, the Tribulation, and the End of the Exile: Restoration Eschatology and the Origin of the Atonement*. Wissenschaftliche Untersuchungen zum Neuen Testament 2/204. Tübingen, Germany: Mohr Siebeck, 2005.

Plantinga, Cornelius. *Not the Way It's Supposed to Be: A Breviary of Sin*. Grand Rapids, MI: Eerdmans, 1995.

Ross, Allen P. *Holiness to the Lord: A Guide to the Exposition of the Book of Leviticus*. Grand Rapids, MI: Baker Academic, 2002.

Rowling, J. K. *Harry Potter and the Sorcerer's Stone*. New York: Scholastic, 1998.

Sanders, James. "The Exile and Canon Formation." In Scott, *Exile: Old Testament*, 37-61.

Scalise, Pamela J. "The End of the Old Testament: Reading Exile in the Hebrew Bible." *Perspectives in Religious Studies* 35 (2008): 163-78.

Schreiner, Thomas R. *1, 2 Peter, Jude*. New American Commentary 37. Nashville: Broadman & Holman, 2003.

———. "Revelation." In *ESV Expository Commentary*. Vol. 12, *Hebrews-Revelation*, edited by Iain M. Duguid, James M. Hamilton, and Jay Sklar, 525-754. Wheaton, IL: Crossway, 2018.

Scott, James M. "Jesus' Vision for the Restoration of Israel as the Basis for a Biblical Theology of the New Testament." In *Biblical Theology: Retrospect and Prospect*, edited by Scott J. Hafemann, 129-43. Downers Grove, IL: InterVarsity Press, 2002.

———, ed. *Exile: A Conversation with N. T. Wright*. Downers Grove, IL: IVP Academic, 2017.

———. *Exile: Old Testament, Jewish, and Christian Conceptions*. Supplements to the Journal for the Study of Judaism. Leiden, The Netherlands: Brill, 1997.

Smith-Christopher, D. L. "Reassessing the Historical and Sociological Impact of the Babylonian Exile (597/587–539 BCE)." In Scott, *Exile: Old Testament*, 7-36.

Snodgrass, Klyne R. "Reading and Overreading the Parables in *Jesus and the Victory of God*." In *Jesus & the Restoration of Israel: A Critical Assessment of N. T. Wright's Jesus and the Victory of God*, edited by Carey C. Newman, 61-76. Downers Grove, IL: InterVarsity Press, 1999.

Steck, Odil Hannes. "Das Problem theologischer Strömungen in nachexilischer Zeit." *Evangelische Theologie* 28 (1968): 445-58.

———. *Israel und das gewaltsame Geschick der Propheten. Untersuchungen zur Überlieferung des deuteronomistischen Geschichtsbildes im Alten Testament, Spätjudentum und Urchristentum*. Wissenschaftliche Monographien zum Alten und Neuen Testament 23. Neukirchen-Vlyun: Neukirchener Verlag, 1967.

Stuart, Douglas K. *Hosea-Jonah*. Word Biblical Commentary 31. Waco, TX: Word Books, 1987.

Suleiman, Susan Rubin. "Introduction." In *Exile and Creativity Signposts, Travelers, Outsiders, Backward Glances*, edited by Susan Rubin Suleiman, 1-8. Durham, NC: Duke University Press, 1998.

Tabori, Paul. *The Anatomy of Exile: A Semantic and Historical Study*. London: Harrap, 1972.

Thielman, Frank. "The Story of Israel and the Theology of Romans 5-8." In *Pauline Theology*, edited by Jouette M. Bassler, David M. Hay, and E. Elizabeth Johnson, 169-95. Minneapolis: Fortress Press, 1991.

Thompson, Alan J. *The Acts of the Risen Lord Jesus: Luke's Account of God's Unfolding Plan*. New Studies in Biblical Theology 27. Downers Grove, IL: InterVarsity Press, 2011.

Tolkien, J. R. R. *The Fellowship of the Ring: Being the First Part of the Lord of the Rings*. Boston: Houghton Mifflin Harcourt, 2012.

———. *The Letters of J. R. R. Tolkien: A Selection*. Edited by Humphrey Carpenter and Christopher Tolkien. Boston: Houghton Mifflin, 2000.

Tozer, A. W. *The Knowledge of the Holy*. 1st HarperCollins gift ed. New York: HarperSanFrancisco, 1992.

von Rad, Gerhard. *Genesis: A Commentary*. Rev. ed. The Old Testament Library. Philadelphia: Westminster Press, 1972.

Waltke, Bruce K., and Cathi J. Fredricks. *Genesis: A Commentary*. Grand Rapids, MI: Zondervan, 2001.

Walton, John H. *Genesis 1 as Ancient Cosmology*. Winona Lake, IN: Eisenbrauns, 2011.

Watts, Rikki E. *Isaiah's New Exodus in Mark*. Biblical Studies Library. Grand Rapids, MI: Baker Books, 2000.

Wilder, William N. *Echoes of the Exodus Narrative in the Context and Background of Galatians 5:18*. Studies in Biblical Literature 23. New York: P. Lang, 2001.

Williamson, Paul R. *Abraham, Israel, and the Nations: The Patriarchal Promise and Its Covenantal Development in Genesis*. Journal for the Study of the Old Testament Supplement Series 315. Sheffield, UK: Sheffield Academic Press, 2000.

Wright, N. T. *Christian Origins and the Question of God*. Vol. 1, *The New Testament and the People of God*. Minneapolis: Fortress Press, 1992.

———. *Christian Origins and the Question of God*. Vol. 2, *Jesus and the Victory of God*. Minneapolis: Fortress Press, 1996.

———. *Christian Origins and the Question of God*. Vol. 3, *The Resurrection of the Son of God*. Minneapolis: Fortress Press, 2003.

———. *Christian Origins and the Question of God*. Vol. 4, *Paul and the Faithfulness of God*. Minneapolis: Fortress Press, 2013.

———. "In Grateful Dialogue: A Response." In *Jesus & the Restoration of Israel: A Critical Assessment of N. T. Wright's Jesus and the Victory of God*, edited by Carey C. Newman, 244-77. Downers Grove, IL: InterVarsity Press, 1999.

———. "New Exodus, New Inheritance: The Narrative Substructure of Romans 3–8." In *Romans and the People of God: Essays in Honor of Gordon D. Fee on the Occasion of His 65th Birthday*, edited by Sven Soderlund and N. T. Wright, 26-35. Grand Rapids, MI: Eerdmans, 1999.

———. "Yet the Sun Will Rise Again: Reflections on the Exile and Restoration in Second Temple Judaism, Jesus, Paul, and the Church Today." In Scott, *Exile: A Conversation*, 19-80.

AUTHOR INDEX

SCRIPTURE INDEX

ESSENTIAL STUDIES IN
BIBLICAL THEOLOGY

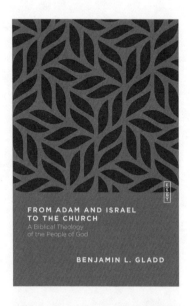

**FROM ADAM AND ISRAEL
TO THE CHURCH**
A Biblical Theology
of the People of God

BENJAMIN L. GLADD

**EXODUS
OLD AND NEW**
A Biblical Theology
of Redemption

L. MICHAEL MORALES

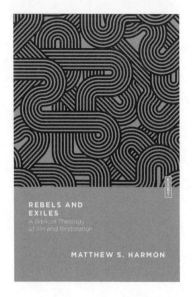

**REBELS AND
EXILES**
A Biblical Theology
of Sin and Restoration

MATTHEW S. HARMON

THE PATH OF FAITH
A Biblical Theology
of Covenant and Law

BRANDON D. CROWE

Finding the Textbook You Need

The IVP Academic Textbook Selector
is an online tool for instantly finding the IVP books
suitable for over 250 courses across 24 disciplines.

ivpacademic.com